BUYING A SHOP

BUYING A SHOP

Extracts from Reviews of earlier editions.

"... one of the best expositions of this intricate subject yet published."

RETAIL CHEMIST

"... If you are pondering how to choose and what to pay – or what to choose and *how* to pay! – this book could help a lot."

C T N

"... sets out a concise, clear and practical plan of action for the would-be buyer."

PROPERTY

"... the author has succeeded in presenting a wealth of concise information of great practical and educational value."

THE PHARMACEUTICAL JOURNAL

"... probably the finest manual ever produced, with so much advice and sound reasoning, in one publication."

THE VALUER

"... whilst this is primarily a business guide for buyers of shops, the sellers have not been forgotten."

THE BOOK EXCHANGE

"... an interesting, well-written book and should be compulsory reading for all pharmaceutical students embarking on a retail career."

THE UNICHEMIST

"a well-written, very readable book for those who are wishing to buy a shop and for their professional advisers." "you can safely recommend it."

LLOYDS BANK STAFF MAGAZINE

"Useful advice on the assessment of goodwill value of a business is given and the dangers of applying any rule-of-thumb formula explained."

CHEMIST AND DRUGGIST

Business books by the same author:
People First in Retail
On Your Head

BUYING A SHOP

—how to choose
—what to pay
—with notes on selling a shop
  and stock control

E. A. Jensen

BUYING A SHOP

Reprinted 1972
2nd Edition (Revised and enlarged) 1973
Reprinted 1973
3rd Edition (Further Revised and enlarged) 1975
Reprinted 1978
4th Edition (enlarged) 1980
5th Edition (Revised and enlarged) 1983
6th Edition (Revised and enlarged) 1986

I.S.B.N. 0-9507437-3-9

Published by
E. A. Jensen

6 Attree Drive, Queen's Park,
Brighton, BN2 2HN Sussex, England
Telephone: Brighton (0273) 605293

Reproduced from copy supplied,
printed and bound in Great Britain
by Billing and Sons Limited,
Worcester

CONTENTS

Buying a Shop

Stock Control

Chapter

AUTHOR'S PREFACE

Every year, many of the several hundred thousand shops in Great Britain change hands; large numbers are bought by people without previous shop-owning experience.

This book is primarily a business guide for **buyers,** but the **seller** has not been forgotten. Here is a practical approach to the problems of what to look for in a shop and to the factors that govern the price of a retail business. Where it is necessary for an understanding of the methods described, the economic theory behind them has been brought in.

Division into chapters has not been simple, as the subjects overlap and are inter-related. The book should therefore be read as a whole and not as a series of separate compartments. Certain topics such as "pure profit" and "the market" are referred to time and again as their importance merits.

The aim has been to offer a concise, clear and *practical* plan of action for the would-be buyer and to suggest, in addition, an attitude of mind. The seller should benefit by studying the buyer's viewpoint and by a fuller understanding of what decides the value of a shop.

In this 6th (1986) edition I have added material extracted and adapted from my book "More Profit from your Stock." This is because I believe any man or woman buying a shop should be familiar with Stock Control Principles.

To take calculated risks is a part of all business life, but we can greatly reduce uncertainty if we will work hard at seeking and interpreting information.

Business conditions can change rapidly and success demands that we keep up to date.

The reader is urged to make sure that in applying examples given in this book he or she uses the latest information available in general and for the particular branch of retailing under consideration. I recommend that you make your own "facts" notebook of turnovers, gross margins, salaries, interest rates, and so forth.

The book is not a series of easy answers, not a set of dogmatic statements; it is intended to outline a reasonable method and approach for those who believe that before the expenditure of money on buying a shop, careful forethought is well worth while. It is also a guide for the seller who wishes to arrive in a reasonable way at the market value of his shop.

E. A. JENSEN,
1986.

special note:—
Figures used to illustrate examples should be updated when necessary and adjusted for the particular trade under consideration.

Chapter 1
INTRODUCTION

For about every one hundred and fifty people in Great Britain there is a retail shop of some kind. These shops range in size from the small "one man" business to the large department store. Total turnover runs into thousands of millions of pounds. Vast sums are invested in stocks of merchandise, in sales equipment, fixtures and so forth, and there are immense assets in the form of property. In addition, there is the goodwill, intangible but valuable, attached to these trading concerns.

Shops are constantly being opened, closed, bought, sold. Ownership of a retail business is often the easiest way for a man with *small* capital to become his own master, and when buying he should, it is clear, make as wise and informed a choice as he can.

When a business changes hands a value has to be placed upon it; there are, of course, other circumstances when a shop has to be valued, but this book is mainly concerned with the buying and selling of a shop and with helping the buyer to a prudent decision. Likewise those wishing to sell can profit by studying the point of view of the prospective buyer.

The calculation of the cash value of a shop cannot be a question only of figures and arithmetic. Naturally it should be done as scientifically as the subject allows, but as we are dealing with practical matters of day-to-day business and as the daily trading of our shops is moulded by human nature and reactions, so the value of a business depends on certain factors which are not easily measured as well as on more concrete and readily discoverable facts. This point will be enlarged upon as we proceed, but let us state now at the outset that to assess the value of a shop you require:

(a) Facts, as many as you can obtain, not only about businesses, but about yourself, and about general economic conditions:

(b) Judgment:

(c) Imagination:

(d) The help, direct and indirect, of the seller (often called the vendor) and of others.

The aim of this book is to suggest a reasonable method for the buyer who wishes to spend his money with wisdom. Please do not expect hard and fast calculations, and do read the book more than once. Be practical, try out the suggested methods of investigation, not only in fireside armchair comfort but by checking and noting facts and conditions on the spot in fair and bad weather; you will then acquire that practical observation of retail conditions which will enable you to study accounts and other figures with true insight. As you persevere, you will find your speed and judgment improve, so you can rapidly separate what is of possible interest to you from what is not. Finally, you are urged to *write down* the answers to the questions I suggest you should ask yourself and others, to be thorough in your self-examination, and to remember that knowledge, including knowledge of yourself, pays well.

We repeat: to place a value on a retail business involves judgment, factual knowledge, imagination, and the co-operation of others. It is necessary to deal with the solid tangible assets such as fixtures and stock, also with the intangibles, in particular goodwill and potential.

In much of this book we shall deal with the intangibles, as these give most difficulty, and especially with the measurement of goodwill and potential. In practice, potential cannot always be clearly separated from goodwill, although in theory the border is well marked. Many of our suggestions will be directed towards finding a reasonable approach to the problem of assessing goodwill, but we shall of necessity bring in the related topics including potential, stock, fixtures and so forth.

A shop should be looked upon as a living organic whole, of which each part influences the others. Thus a gross excess of stock can adversely influence goodwill value, unsuitable fixtures may depress the market price, and so on.

The valuation of stock is normally in the main scientific, but with an element of opinion and judgment. In contracts drawn up for the sale of shops

2

it is often stated that the purchaser shall buy good clean saleable stock; now there must be, in most stocks, items on the condition of which opinion can vary, and hence the value of appointing independent valuers whose judgment shall be final and binding on both sides. Goodwill and potential can only be valued through a combination of opinion and science, the element of judgment being more pronounced than in the case of stock. Fixtures and fittings tend to occupy an intermediate position as regards the relative proportions of judgment and science involved in their valuation.

Our aim is to place on a rational basis the valuation of the intangibles, but we must stress that this does not permit of a dogmatic approach. We shall put forward what it is hoped will be accepted as a reasonable method of procedure, but *no rigid formulae*. Our object is to provide a *consistent technique,* which takes into account the almost infinite variety of retail business in this country. Our shops express our national individuality, and in studying them we study also human nature. Quick "rule of thumb" methods will not do.

We try to make clearer the principles of investigating and arriving at a fair price for retail businesses. No easy way is shown, because there is no substitute for study, hard work, and a measure of imagination. The exceptional man may appear to show what is called a "flair" for picking a good business but, by and large, what passes for "flair" is a combination of less dramatic qualities within the reach of most of us. If we work on a sound basis perhaps we, too, shall develop something of a "flair".

Study of the principles outlined here is meant to help, in judging the value of a shop, all those who own or hope to own a retail business, and to suggest rational means of investigating a shop considered for purchase. As we have said before, those wishing to sell can doubtless profit by studying the method of those who aim to buy. What is required then is a process, a way of bringing some order and balance into what can appear a haphazard and frustrating job – that of choosing and deciding upon the value of a shop.

ABOUT THE AUTHOR:

The author served his apprenticeship in retail pharmacy in Lancashire during the depression of the 30's. After further retail experience he spent about four years (with an interlude of over six years in the army), in the sales administration of a large manufacturing pharmaceutical company.

After the war Mr. Jensen was, for several years, Managing Director of a wholesale sundries business in the South; then followed about 14 years with a large specialist firm of valuers and transfer agents in London. He has handled hundreds of business sales/purchases.

In 1968 Mr. Jensen set up as a self-employed business consultant based on Brighton, and in the course of this work he has devoted much of his time in recent years to retail. He lectures on business and management topics and has made a special study of Attitude Training. He is very keen to promote the idea that PEOPLE, rather than things, are of prime importance.

Chapter 2

GOODWILL

Goodwill is a familiar term to the business man; it may be associated with a name, a trademark, a person, a firm, a trading position. When a business is sold, or its ownership varies, for example on the introduction of a new partner, an assessment of the value of the goodwill is normally called for.

Goodwill is a special form of asset, intangible, variable, often of great value, and coming in the field of applied economics. Market laws apply to the valuation of goodwill, and the demand for a particular business or type of business in relation to the number of such businesses available, will govern the price at any given time. When we come to a closer study of the subject, especially when we consider how intimately it is linked with ideas of profit, we shall be drawn into fields of economic theory much wider than we had perhaps expected.

A simple truth to be kept before us all the time is that *value is a measure of the relation between supply and demand, and value expressed in terms of money is price.* If there is no one able and willing to buy, then an article has no value in this sense, however much may have been spent in producing it, however much its owner treasures it. Values vary from time to time and we therefore stress that while the goodwill of a business might have cost, say, £50,000 to buy, this is not necessarily the value under different circumstances at another time. *The current market is the governing factor*, and those who wish to deal realistically with business must keep this always before them.

One important object of this book is to define goodwill as we shall use the term, then to discuss those factors which go to build it up or which detract from it. After preparing the way, we can discuss a reasonable method for valuing goodwill, linking theory and practical business affairs.

The subject is such that one can indicate an approach, an attitude to the question, rather than offer a solution in concrete terms. *We are not weighing tons of coal or counting units of money; we are trying to place a value on something which can vary from time to time, from place to place, and according to the desires of buyer and seller.*

Nevertheless we must unite theory and practice, and try to deal with the problem, faced every day by someone, of placing a price on the intangible goodwill.

Should you doubt the importance of the topic, consider the number of retail businesses which to your own knowledge change hands every year, the number which open or close. Think of the number of shop owners who die, the many people who in your experience break up old partnerships or enter into new ones. With most of these events are involved valuations of stock, fixtures, equipment *and goodwill.* In the things valued on such occasions we have goods which can be measured, weighed, and priced in fair relation to market value; we also have goodwill, invisible and potent. The goodwill of a business is often the measure of a man's life work, the result of his business acumen, and the key to the future.

In a case which came before the courts in 1810, goodwill was defined as "the probability that the old customers will resort to the old place" (Lord Eldon). This is the basic definition we propose to use although we shall examine and enlarge on this statement; we understand it to mean that *goodwill is the probability that the amount of business which has been done by a particular shop in the past will continue to be done by that shop in the future.* By the "amount of business done" we shall understand the "amount of profit made".

Chapter 3

RISK, PROFIT AND GOODWILL

We should now give close study to certain implications of our definition of goodwill. To revert to Lord Eldon, it is first of all most important to underline the term *probability*. It is clear, by the very inclusion of the word "probability" in the definition, that goodwill is by nature linked with uncertainty. We have referred to the "amount of profit made" and our suggested method of assessing goodwill will show that we have to enter into the consideration of profits, not only of gross profit and net profit but also of *pure profit*.

We can look ahead a little by stressing the relation between goodwill and profit. In very broad terms, and with some important qualifications, the absence of pure profit (to be defined in our next chapter), means absence of goodwill. This follows from the idea that profit is the return to risk-bearing. We reason that profit implies risk-bearing and uncertainty, and that goodwill involves profit. So goodwill and risk must be associated and we can see the link with Lord Eldon's definition which included the word "probability". *Probability suggests some measure of uncertainty and risk, these imply profit, and profit normally governs goodwill values.*

It will not be found sufficient for the prudent would-be purchaser merely to satisfy himself that a specified pure profit has been made; he will require to study *how* it has been made. Such an analysis will assist in a cross-check of the facts, in encouraging close study of the proposition, and in helping a buyer to look into the future by gaining a clear picture of the past.

It is emphasised that goodwill as we have described it is concerned with the probability of keeping in the future, customers who have dealt with a particular business in the past. This is of prime importance to the buyer of a business. A careful division should be made between goodwill, which is based on the likelihood of a future continuance of past and proved performance, and *potential,* which is a forecast of future possibilities not already exploited in the shop concerned.

7

Briefly, to buy a poor unprofitable shop for what you think you can make of it must be something of a gamble, a gamble which, if successful, may provide you with results to enable you to sell goodwill at a later date. On the other hand, to buy goodwill is to have faith that past results will continue.

If, therefore, you are thinking of purchasing goodwill, you should see clearly that you are estimating the prospects of being able to extend into the future the success which has been achieved in the past by the vendor of the goodwill. The element of risk may be so small as to be almost non-existent, yet it may be so large as to give you little assurance for the future. But some risk there is bound to be; to weigh it in the balance you should, as a careful business man, investigate thoroughly the many aspects of the proposition you are considering. However, let us emphasise the fact that *without accepting risk one cannot in fairness expect profit;* conversely, to take a risk which offers you in return no chance of profit, is not prudent business.

We shall deal later with suggested ways of tackling the problem; at this point it is not out of place to insert a caution sometimes necessary to people who are over-zealous and exacting. Through too much investigation, or by tardy decision, many seekers after businesses repeatedly lose what could have been their ideal shop. If you know what to look for, an investigation need not in normal cases be long drawn out. A seller will not always be waiting your pleasure, and often a too-theoretical buyer reaches at last his carefully pondered decision, only to find that someone more rapid and perhaps more skilled, has come before him. One can never cover every eventuality and some risk must be accepted; the skill is in finding a sensible balance between rashness and over-caution.

A prime cure for indecision is knowledge. To the well-schooled business man most problems should fall within a pattern of likely answers; few should be entirely new. Past experience and a definite procedure as suggested in this book will be found to help in developing decision where this is lacking. For those not trained in business it is important to have a clear plan of action and a method of building up the necessary store of knowledge.

Chapter 4

PURE PROFIT AND GOODWILL

Before going on to a study of those factors which may give rise to goodwill, we should develop the theme that goodwill is associated with profit and therefore with risk-bearing and uncertainty.

There is no need to discuss the relation between profit and risk-bearing. Reference to a standard work on general economics would satisfy the reader that as, in general terms, wages are the return to labour, rent the return to land, and interest the return to capital, so profit is the return to or reward for risk-bearing and the acceptance of uncertainty. There is profit only if a venture is successful; the result of risk-taking and uncertainty might well be loss.

After this brief summary, the next problem we must face is the special interpretation given in this book to the term "profit". The ideas of gross profit and net profit are so commonly understood as not to need explanation here, but for the understanding and valuing of goodwill a special viewpoint on profit is to be examined.

Let us pause to ask ourselves why a purchaser buys a retail business. For our immediate purpose we are concerned only with the monetary aspects of his decision to buy a shop; we will not venture into the moral, ethical and other motives which are involved.

The immediate aim of most buyers of shops is to make money. The purchaser seeks a gross profit, a net profit and, as we intend to show, a pure profit.

By pure profit we mean a return above what the buyer could earn as the manager of a business similar to the one he is buying and having (but without any investment of money) substantially the work to do which he would have to do as *owner*-manager. Furthermore we must allow for what can be obtained as interest, in a "safe" investment, on the money needed to buy any particular shop we are considering.

Here is a simple illustration. A business is showing a net profit of £20,000 per anum to a vendor working in it himself as owner-manager; the price at which it is being sold is £60,000, this including stock, fixtures, fittings, etc., goodwill and lease. Let us assume the salary of a manager in this type and size of business to be £8,000 per annum; let us also take it that the current Building Society interest rate is 10 per cent to investors. In this example the pure profit would be £20,000 less £8,000 and less 10 per cent of £60,000. This pure profit would be £20,000 minus £14,000; hence £6,000 per annum is the return on risk-bearing.

Now if the £20,000 were the net return to an owner not working in the business, i.e. after he had paid someone else a normal management salary, then the pure profit figure would be £14,000 that is, £20,000 less 10 per cent of £60,000.

With an owner devoting some time only to the business, a proportionate allowance should be made. Time and work directly and indirectly devoted to the business must be taken into account and a cash value placed on them.

We have now arrived at the basic idea of pure profit, starting from a given net profit. But our net profit figure will itself require close inspection and we shall, in a later chapter, need to examine this net profit and also the gross profit; otherwise we are taking our pure profit figure from information which is not in itself reasonably definite and understood. For the moment, shall we consider further the implications of pure profit defined as "the return to the owner of a business after allowing for his own salary as manager and for a current safe return in the form of interest on the total capital invested"?*

---

*Total capital invested in a shop is the price for which it can be sold as a going concern *in the current market*. If the freehold is bought this should be dealt with separately from a return on capital viewpoint and in arriving at the profit figure allowance should be made for an appropriate rent equivalent.

Our reasons for preferring the pure profit idea as an aid in valuing goodwill are as follows:

It is against normal human nature to invest money only to obtain a return equal to that obtainable without investment. Why should a man spend, say, £40,000 on a business which can on past results give him as working owner-manager only a return of the same amount he could receive as an employee-manager? Furthermore, why should he also sacrifice interest which could be drawn by him while he worked as an employee taking none of the risk of ownership?

Some men are ready to work as owners for a return only equal to or even less than what they could earn from others and from safe investment of their capital. Such men are prepared to pay a premium, as it were, to be their own master, to make some sacrifice for not being an employee. These men are in a minority but may have some effect in the direction of keeping goodwill figures above what they would otherwise be. As we shall see later, the condition of the market at any given time will be the final arbiter of goodwill values.

To repeat, goodwill values are based on proved performance *in the past,* that is, on past figures, on the probability that customers already obtained will continue to patronize the business. The risk to be considered in relation to goodwill is whether these customers will in fact be retained, and this uncertainty is to be carefully distinguished from the doubt as to whether new customers can be attracted, that is, from speculation on the potential of a business.

If you are paying for potential, at any rate be clear what you are doing and avoid the hazy mixing together of past and future. The valuation of goodwill is complex enough without, at this stage, bringing in *potential,* which, as previously explained, is quite another thing. More will be said of potential later, when we shall have to decide whether we can in practice always completely separate goodwill from potential.

The comment we have made in our last paragraph might at first appear to be inconsistent with the previous advice not to mix goodwill and potential; what we wish to stress is that you should know when there is included in a

11

purchase price some payment for potential even if the amount paid for potential cannot be separated from the total price.

Note: From what has been written in this chapter, it will be clear that higher management salaries and/or higher rates of interest would tend to depress goodwill values:- if other things remained equal. And conversely.

But in practical economics "other things" rarely remain equal; we can easily get involved in a mass of variables.

You will be wise to study how salaries and interest rates vary as compared with prices and profits. You could do this both generally and in the type of shop which you are considering.

Chapter 5
PROFIT: HOW IT ARISES

We have referred to gross profit, to net profit, to pure profit. Now it is necessary to study how profit arises, since profit is the corner-stone in our assessment of goodwill value. Let us turn briefly to the first principles of business accounting as applied to retail trade.

The gross profit is calculated as the difference between (the value of stock at the beginning of the period plus purchases at cost price during the period) *and* (the value of stock at the close of the period plus sales at retail price). *For accountancy purposes* stock is customarily valued at actual cost or current market cost price, whichever is the lower. When, on the other hand, a business is bought, the purchaser usually pays the current market cost price, that is, the price he would have to pay for the goods in stock if he had to buy them from the usual suppliers at the time of his purchasing the shop.

From the gross profit arrived at by the process described above, net profit is reached by deducting all expenses of a current nature, for example, rent, rates, wages, bank charges, insurances, postages, telephone charges and so forth. By contrast, capital laid out, for example, in the purchase of a new delivery van, would not be included as a charge against profits, although the petrol, oil, repairs and other running expenses would be so included.

Having decided upon the net profit, we can ascertain the pure profit by the method outlined in a previous chapter.

It will be imperative to study in detail a typical Profit and Loss Account and Balance Sheet. Figures can be read in varying ways and must be correctly interpreted for a true picture of the profit (gross, net or pure) of a business and of the assets and liabilities to be seen.

The entries in the Profit and Loss Account are, however, principally reflections of real costs as distinct from money costs and the factors related to these real costs need analysis. For instance, rent may appear as £1,500 per annum and this cash amount should be considered as a reflection of the position and nature of the property involved; wages are a mirror of the local and national labour and staff situation; insurance costs are a measure of the type of stock held, and so forth.

It is logical to turn now to those factors which, by making one business more profitable or less profitable than another, or for other reasons, influence goodwill values.

Chapter 6

TRADING POSITION, PROFIT AND GOODWILL

The first factor we turn to is the geographical position of the business; it is of supreme importance.

We shall need to ask ourselves:
(1) How far the position of the business under review influences the takings?
(2) Whether the advantages or disadvantages of the position are likely to change through outside affairs and what is the degree of risk involved?
(3) Is the position such as to suggest potential?

The site of the business should be looked at from various angles, each with its own significance to goodwill. Start with the broad aspect of the relation between the region or town where the business is situated and the country as a whole. Is the business in a district which is relatively prosperous, and if so, are these favourable conditions likely to continue? Some investigation of the general economic and social features of the area must be made, and we should try to decide whether present conditions will improve, deteriorate, or remain about the same.

Let us always remember, however, that we are concerned *with one particular shop* and that it may be doing well in an area which is on the whole depressed, or may be faring badly in a district where trade otherwise is good. At this stage it is worth stressing that information of a general nature has its value and purpose, but that we shall need to seek the individual facts about the particular business we are analysing.

Other things being equal, we would normally value higher the goodwill of a business in an area where general trade prospects are apparently good, than that of one where the reverse is true. Having formed an overall picture of the

15

area or town, we should then survey the shop's more immediate district or neighbourhood. We may need to study a suburb or a new estate which possibly, for special local reasons, differs from the general picture in being relatively prosperous or depressed.

After examining the county and town, then the suburb or estate, we narrow our investigation to the parade which includes the shop we are assessing; we examine the trading fortunes and prospects of the shops in the group. A shop may (because a factory nearby is doing well), be prosperous despite a general depression in the estate or town as a whole.

Here are practical examples. The Midland area, Birmingham, Nottingham, Leicester, has never known depression so severe as that suffered by the Lancashire cotton towns, South Wales, or the North-East coast. In bad times one may find that street market shops do *relatively* well as customers are driven to these often cheaper sources of supply. Certain shops indulging in cut-price tactics find their business stimulated by general depression and money shortage, and their relative prosperity reduced when purchasers have less need to count their money so carefully.

The lesson to be drawn from these considerations is that a business must be weighed up on its own unique qualities. No two businesses can be exactly the same; apart from other variations they must occupy different trading positions. Our plan will be to work from the general to the particular and to end with a study of the one business under review.

Let us imagine we stand before the shop we are studying. We may have decided that the area around the business is prosperous and that this state of affairs seems likely to continue, that the part of the country as a whole is sound and shows no special vulnerability to any trade recession which could reasonably be expected. What immediate factors should we ponder?

The basis of the trade of our shop is obviously the number of customers patronizing it and the amount each spends. The average retail shop is dependent on passing trade and residential trade in varying proportions and these proportions are very important. Here we must state, as a very broad general rule only, that the more a business draws its customers from *casual* passing shoppers, the less will its goodwill rest upon the personality of the proprietor and staff. Conversely, the fate of a business primarily dependent on regular repeat customers from a surrounding residential district will tend to hinge on the personal qualities of the owner and staff.

From these general truths, which do not apply in every individual case, we may conclude that, other things being equal, goodwill of a personal nature, i.e., related to a regular residential trade, can be more quickly lost through purely personal or character defects than can passing trade goodwill. Passing trade largely dependent upon efficient stocking and business management may be more readily lost through lack of purely business acumen. As extremes, we could contrast a kiosk in the City of London, where position, stock, speed, are almost everything, with a business in a village or in an estate or block of flats, where personal contact counts for so much.

The position of a shop is important in several ways apart from the relation the site bears to customers. We must also consider position in relation to means of transport, competitors, suppliers, supporting shops, and other local features which may attract people to, or repel them from, the area of the business under review.

Each of these factors and others which will suggest themselves to you, should be considered from the point of view: Has it contributed to the profit and goodwill, and if so is the contribution so trivial as to be negligible or so important as to warrant close analysis?

As an example, a business may have derived much trade from its location near a railway station or a bus stop; the latter is much more likely to be moved than the former, although stations are on occasion closed down; or again, a shop may be located opposite a vacant site due for re-development; here any trade obtained in the last few years may well increase substantially or slightly, according to the type of rebuilding which takes place – a new block of flats could by itself support some types of shop, while other forms of building might offer fewer potential customers.

The geographical relation between shops and wholesalers, or manufacturers, can be of great importance. Many small businesses, especially in or near large towns, live almost from day to day on stocks held by a nearby wholesaler, thus reducing the working capital needed and in some ways the amount of skill required in buying and stock-keeping. This proximity to suppliers would be an influence towards increasing the goodwill value.

Shop purchasers usually give some thought to the question of competitors (see Chapter 10) and their distance from a shop under review. Many buyers are filled with the desire to have no opposition near them. Here we may digress for a moment to emphasise that no business is in fact unopposed; *any alternative way in which money can be spent by the available customers is competition.* In the end, all goods and services on the market compete for the public's money and another grocer is not the only competitor the grocer needs to consider. For the moment, however, let us confine ourselves to thinking of competition from another shop or shops in the same trade as the one whose goodwill we are considering. If there is now a great distance (in relation to the population to be served), between the shop and its nearest competitor, *new opposition* may be much more likely than if the present opposition is fairly near and it has been established firmly for some years. A goodwill value resulting from profits achieved in the face of keen competition may be more stable, more likely to persist, than one built up from circumstances where there is an obvious opening for a new competitor.

It is vital to study closely the position and nature of competition. The type of pitfall which may arise is instanced by the following. Imagine a shop with steady returns and profits and with general circumstances pointing to a continuance of such returns and profits. The nearest competitive business has perhaps changed ownership quite recently and the new man might be about the same type as his predecessor. He could, however, be much more, or much less, efficient and likeable, and this can make a substantial variation in the future returns of "our" shop. We must especially consider whether a nearby competitor is inefficient or unpopular and whether he is likely soon to be replaced by a more dangerous opponent.

A part of our local investigation on this question of position must therefore be the closest scrutiny of the position, type, and history of the shops most likely to compete. This aspect can hardly be over-stressed, yet many buyers are content with a hurried survey. Care is most essential.

It may be objected, indeed we have ourselves pointed out, that if a prospective buyer investigates too long, he can very well lose the desired business to someone who acts more quickly. This is true, but the time needed for a full investigation is not of necessity long, *provided adequate thought has been given in advance.* **Many buyers seem to spend too long looking at figures which are history, not enough on market investigation of aspects which affect future trade.**

Most buyers have at any rate some broad ideas as to the location and type of business they seek. If they have not this very minimum clear view of their desires, it is suggested they give serious thought to the matter. Of businesses on the market at any time, a majority can probably be rejected for reasons not connected with the local factors at present under review. If for example, a business is sought in say Sussex, and it must have living accommodation on the premises, a garage, a garden, and also must be in a coastal town, then an initial survey will very likely rule out most shops.

A buyer can save time by having in his mind, or very much better, *on paper,* a clear definition of the business which he would buy subject to a final check on those factors which can only be considered in relation to one specific shop. Then when a proposition comes under examination a great deal of preliminary work has already been done; the locality and opposition may be known in advance and all that is required is perhaps a final check of any recent changes, followed by detailed inspection of the business itself. In other words preparation beforehand can often give speed without loss of thoroughness.

It is in practice found very often that sound businesses tend to go quickly to knowledgeable buyers who can decide rapidly because they have forearmed themselves with all possible obtainable data. If your needs are specific then you will probably know at least one business you would wish to buy if it were for sale. Should your requirements not yet be definite, then it is suggested you do your best to make them so and thus help your decisiveness and speed.

Provided you know *where* approximately you wish to buy, you can profit by absorbing local knowledge.

Read the local and county newspapers. Visit the village or town or suburb as often as you can and at as many different times as possible. Try to inspect on varying days and under diverse conditions. Study the shopping pattern, that is, ascertain which is the busier side of a road and why, the movement of the shoppers, and so forth. Does wet weather make a difference? Some arcade shops are most sensitive to weather conditions and it may happen that rain at 2 o'clock on Saturdays can prevent many people from coming out to shop at all, while rain at 3.30 may send much business to the arcade from shoppers caught in the nearby exposed streets. Consider the influence also of bus shelters, pedestrian crossings, one-way streets. In relation to profit and goodwill, trading position is vital; please study the notes at the end of the chapter.

A full investigation of the level of the prosperity in a given area would require much time and expense. What is needed for our present purpose is an indication of some of the main pointers to be examined by someone considering whether to buy a business in a specific location.

First of all consider the amount of unemployment and whether this is likely to be permanent or temporary. Examine average earnings, the type of job held, the number of cars, television sets, telephones, luxury shops.

Study the effect on the area of previous national booms or slumps. Does the locality depend for much of its employment and spending power on armament programmes; is the work varied or could a fall in sales of one particular type of merchandise have grave effects?

Statistical information can be obtained from a local guide book or from the Chamber of Commerce. Do not, however, rely over-much on purely paper investigations; **there is no real substitute for a slow** *walk,* **I stress** *walk,* **around the district.** It takes surprisingly little time to survey an area of say half a mile by half a mile in most towns. First go round quickly and gain a general picture, perhaps by car, but then follow up thoroughly *on foot.* Note the types and conditions of houses and shops, especially of directly competitive businesses of the trade you are investigating. Notice the cars, the television aerials and the telephones, the clothes and the general appearance of the residents and passers-by. Are there empty shops and do they appear to have been empty for long? Dust and the dates of advertising announcements in windows of empty premises can be very revealing.

It should be remembered that our present remarks are concentrated on the spending power and prosperity of the district, and you should, (as part of your overall analysis of the district), also check on other aspects such as the shopping routes taken by the public.

Ask questions, make casual purchases from a few shops of varying trades and learn what you can from the shopkeepers. Note how many factories or warehouses are in the district and check on office buildings and so on.

A morning should often be ample to carry out the suggestions in this chapter; you will speed up with practice. Much of the "figure" data can be obtained in advance of your visit, but do *walk* your area, as it is amazing what you can overlook from a car even in a slow drive.

We have referred to an area of say a half mile square, but the space to be covered must naturally vary according to the type of business you are investigating. The distance should normally take you at least as far as the nearest competitor in each direction; in some cases this could mean a journey of several miles. In most instances, however, with the ordinary type of shop, the area to be covered is not large. If you are checking on a business in a small town or village it is useful to visit larger neighbouring towns which draw customers from the area concerned.

The position factors outlined in this chapter should be studied with alert curiosity and it is suggested you add other factors concerned with position as these come to your mind. By developing a technique on the general lines we have put forward, in relation to one area, you will find your skill and speed grow if this "know-how" has to be employed in respect of other localities.

Here are some trading-position points to consider when you investigate an established business or think of opening a new one. Add any additional factors you think of which are special to a site or a business you are considering.

CHECK: How is the position related to:

Traffic lights?

Pedestrian crossings?

Any curve of the street?

Shops on the concave side tend to have a smaller frontage and to get wider towards the back of the premises, but such positions are usually better seen by shoppers.

A shop on the convex side normally has a wider frontage narrowing to the back of the premises and is often not so well seen. Naturally the degree of curve governs its effect.

Sunshine and shade?

Islands, guard rails etc.?

Bus stops?

Bus and railway stations, ferry terminals, sea and airports etc.?

Prevailing wind and rain?

Access bays, service roads, other delivery and despatch arrangements?

The middle and ends of the street? For example, is the position off centre? Consider the pros and cons of a corner site.

Other leading shops, supporting shops, competitive shops?

Car parking and cars generally? Cars parked in front of a shop can hide displays from across the road and can make crossing more hazardous.

Living accommodation in the form of flats, houses etc.?

Any need to expand the shop area in future?

Is traffic one way (if so, for how long), or likely to become one way?

What has been or is likely to be the result? Make similar checks about a pedestrian precinct or street.

In the case of one-way traffic outside the town centre, is the one-way flow into or away from the centre? Are shoppers for your trade more likely to stop on the way in or out and is there somewhere for them to park easily?

How many cars, how much public transport and how many pedestrians (and what types) pass the shop? Take counts at intervals on different days and under varied conditions. Don't just count customers, but all who pass; remember the importance of potential.

Development plans under the Town and Country Planning legislation should be studied; refer to the Local Authority.

Remember the tendency is for shops to get bigger and, as already mentioned, look at the site from this aspect. The number of shops is tending to fall.

Check on the width of street and pavement and ask yourself whether the shop is prominent and distinctive or could it be made so? Is the parade drab and uniform?

Look critically at the shop front. Does it help or hinder business? Study it from a distance as well as close at hand. The shop front might be much more important in a main town centre position than in a village. Does the front attract, does it identify the business; if not can this be remedied? Has the shop individuality?

Consider, and here you need expert advice, the advantages and snags of sites on a slope.

Look ahead and consider the growth of out of town and neighbourhood shopping centres. Will town centres deteriorate or will they meet the challenge? Visit as many and as varied new developments as you can, both within and outside town centres. Study how town centres are employing shopping precincts and other ideas to maintain and enhance their attractiveness.

YOUR NOTES:-

Chapter 7
PERSONALITY, PROFIT AND GOODWILL

Human relations enter into all business transactions, and we use various means of communication such as the letter, the telephone, the face to face meeting, the leaflet, the press advertisement. At present retail business is carried on usually to a dominant degree by direct face to face contact, so that this aspect of personality is of prime importance to the retailer. In a shop the personal reputation and acceptability of proprietor and staff can often have immense influence on the making of pure profit or loss, and therefore on goodwill.

As a general principle, the significance of an attractive personality is inversely to the "passing trade" value of the shop site. Some shops live on being able to supply without delay the goods demanded, that is on efficient stock-keeping and on quick service. What the customer thinks of the owner and staff as people is not of main importance. Many examples of such businesses are to be seen in London, a typical instance being the quick-service cigarette and sweet shop found situated say near the tube station entrance. Customers have little time for anything but being served.

Other shops depend very much on the attitude of the regular customers to the proprietor and staff as well as on the service given over many years. The likeability of staff and owner can decide the fortunes of such businesses.

The majority of shops depend on a varying mixture of the qualities referred to in the last two paragraphs. With an owner of outstanding personality (which also embraces personal efficiency and service) and in addition a strategic trading position, we can expect a business to be numbered amongst the most successful; with a bad site and poor personality, failure often threatens.

The prospective buyer of a business must form a reasoned view of the extent to which any goodwill has resulted from the type of personality of the seller, and he should weigh up with as little bias as possible his own chances of maintaining or increasing the goodwill based on such personality. The extent to which the investigation is necessary will naturally depend on the degree to which personality affects the profit of the business concerned.

What we term personality in business results from temperament, knowledge, experience and character, all of which must be considered in relation to the job in which they are employed. Thus in deciding whether to purchase a business with a large element of personal goodwill, the investigator should satisfy himself on the facts of his own personality and consider them in comparison with the personality of the vendor.

Even a man of high integrity and great charm can, through lack of specialised knowledge and experience, quickly destroy the goodwill of a business. To be pleasant, reliable, honest, is not enough if knowledge is deficient. As a very simple example of this we might take the case of an amateur photographer, reasonably proficient in "still" photography, taking over a business with a large cine film and apparatus connection. Such a business can be speedily ruined if in the wrong hands technically, and to regain lost custom may be costly if not impossible. The reader will doubtless quickly think of his own examples of what we have referred to.

We come naturally to the tentative conclusion that goodwill, reflecting pure profit and the likelihood of this profit continuing, is not only a question of the business itself but of the personalities of buyer and seller. We must ask ourselves this: does the goodwill of the same business vary in relation to different buyers? If it does, and we may be forced to think so, then how does the result link up with the law of the market, of supply and demand? Is something for sale (in this case a shop) worth in fact only what someone is ready, willing and able to pay for it? Is this theory borne out in practice? We come to these questions again in later chapters.

Chapter 8

PEOPLE, CONNECTION, PROFIT AND GOODWILL

The profit of any business springs from its customers or clients; it must have a market for its goods or services. This market is what is usually termed "connection" and consists of people who trade with a shop because of its convenient situation, the personality of the owner and staff, the service, the prices, the variety of goods and so forth. In this chapter we discuss certain wider aspects of connection which are sometimes overlooked.

The connection of a business may be split into four main elements:

(a) The relation between the business and the people to whom it supplies goods and/or services;

(b) The relation with suppliers of goods to the business;

(c) Other relations, not so direct as under *(a)* or *(b),* but also important. Under this heading we may include relations with:

    (i)   other shopkeepers in the area;

    (ii)   the landlord of the property if it is on lease;

    (iii)   any local government official or department within whose orbit the shop's activities or part of them may come, Consumer Protection Department (formerly Trading Standards Department and before that Weights and Measures Department), Customs and Excise Officer, and so on;

    (iv)   the officers of any trade or professional body to which the owner may belong; and

    (v)   bank manager, accountant, solicitor, consultant.

(d) The relations between owner, directors, partners, staff.

The relation under heading *(a)* hardly calls for discussion here; it is something which is constantly in the mind of the owner of a business. Certain of the items under heading *(c)* are often not given enough attention, but a moment's thought will suggest how important they are.

The main purpose of this chapter is to emphasise that the class of relationship under heading *(b)* must be closely watched; it can have a powerful influence on the goodwill, i.e., on the likelihood that present customers will continue to patronize the shop.

The vendor of a business may have been trading there for twenty or thirty years, and have had unusual credit granted to him by suppliers who knew him well, or been given other special concessions which can make a substantial difference to the capital needed and to the general conduct of the enterprise. A newcomer taking over may find reluctance on the part of suppliers to continue these helpful practices. Sometimes suppliers may take the opportunity given by a change of ownership to tighten up their business arrangements with the shop; there may arise a chain of events such as that now described.

Consider the buyer who barely manages to finance his purchase and then has very little remaining capital. Suppose the rate of stock turnover for the business has in the past been high, that is, a low average stock has been held in relation to sales. Let us imagine that this turnover rate has been helped by supply to the shop of goods on sale or return at special periods, for example, at Christmas, and that the retailer has had further help in the form of exceptionally quick delivery service and the willingness to supply small quantities at a time without charging higher rates. The supplier may also have granted lengthy credit and in effect therefore given the trader an interest-free loan. If these facilities, or some of them, are withdrawn or curtailed, the buyer of the business may find his limited capital insufficient to permit him to carry enough stock to give the service of his predecessor. Sales fall, ready money becomes even scarcer, and as this happens, more and more suppliers may demand quick payment, or payment in advance. The position of the new owner becomes worse and worse and the trouble is incurable if he cannot either obtain credit or raise more money.

The lesson is that a buyer should check up as to whether a business has owed some of its profits to conditions which may not apply to him. What is the probability that past profit will be maintained? Always bear this question in mind and link it with your own financial position in relation to a particular business, as well as with other personal circumstances referred to in this book.

Once more we stress the importance of adequate preparation in advance. It means, among other things, finding out *before* you buy what help (should you need it) you can expect from suppliers and from other business connections such as your bank.

The Value of People

We have referred to the personality of owner and staff. It is important to assess staff and arrive at some idea of their value in the business; this can be considered in the light of *present* worth and *potential* worth.

Clearly we must also make an assessment of the likelihood of staff staying on and for how long. The importance of whether the staff will continue varies with the type of shop and the customer, etc./staff relationship. Where personality is least important, loss of staff will usually be of least damage. Take legal advice if there are staff you do not wish to retain.

Find out all you can about the staff of a shop you are examining, in addition to *general* facts on the ratio of wages to turnover, rate of staff turnover (showing average length of service) and the reasons for this.

Individual data should cover
AGE (which might affect value, or be neutral)
LENGTH OF SERVICE
TRAINING
PERSONALITY (and in particular *attitudes)*
ABILITY AND POTENTIAL
RELATIONSHIP WITH CUSTOMERS (in the broadest sense), WITH SUPPLIERS, AND WITH OTHERS (including the OWNER).

Look at all these, and at other points which might occur to you, in respect of the shop, *(a)* as it *is,* and *(b)* as it *might* be.

In the unlikely event of there being no unused staff ability, staff worth is reflected in the profits, which are taken into account in valuing the business goodwill. If there is unused staff ability, this can be regarded as a part of any *potential* of the business and could help promote *greater* profitability in the future. Alternatively, it could increase the chances of maintaining past profits and therefore make goodwill more solid.

Although we might not be able to place an exact cash value on staff, we must understand their value in any shop. We must remember that investment in people, in developing and training, can be the most productive of all investments for *all* involved. And this consideration of human values reinforces the opinion that there is no formula for goodwill.

YOUR NOTES:-

Chapter 9

SOCIAL AMENITIES, PROFIT AND GOODWILL

We have suggested that the goodwill value of a business depends on past profit and the prospect of this continuing; but the price paid in the market will finally depend on the appeal of *the business as a whole* to prospective purchasers. **Would-be buyers will be influenced by other factors in addition to purely financial ones.**

A group of such influences which are not purely financial, (although they might also have financial angles), may be considered under the broad heading of social factors. Other things being equal, the price of a business will tend to be higher, the market for it wider, if it can offer some or all of the following; naturally buyers will not all think alike on the importance of each point:

(1) Living accommodation on the premises; the value of this will vary with the number and size of rooms, condition, convenience of layout, inclusion of a garden and garage, and so forth;

(2) The availability of schools in the neighbourhood;

(3) The convenience of transport;

(4) Ease of access to amusements, sports, libraries, and other shops;

(5) Proximity to a large city;

(6) Nearness to the coast or countryside;

(7) The general standing of the district;

(8) Climate;

(9) ....

(10) ....

(11) ....

(etc.)

This list is not complete; the reader is left to add social factors of his own.

The important point from the buying or selling aspect is that some or all of these social influences will affect the market value of a shop. The less a buyer is concerned with the amenities, the greater is his chance of buying a business at a so-called "low" price. The more a seller can offer in the way of social attractions the greater normally is his chance of selling.

Once more we should stress that every shop is unique, as is every buyer. The interaction between one business and one buyer is the final measure of its value. It is also worth emphasising that if the market is reasonably "perfect" (please see ahead) then at any time the various advantages and disadvantages of our shop will in fact be weighed up and rule the price. *In short, only ignorance of the market on the part of buyer or seller or both can produce what may be truly termed a "bargain" for the buyer or a windfall for the seller.*

What do we mean by the terms "market" and "perfect market"? A market for businesses, as for anything else, is a collection of sellers and buyers in touch with one another; they may be meeting face to face, by letter, by telephone, in fact by a whole variety of different forms of contact. For there to be a market we must have prospective sellers and would-be purchasers. If every prospective buyer knows at any time what goods are being offered for sale, their respective merits, and the prices being asked, and if at the same time prospective sellers know what buyers are available, prices being obtained, and what the demand is, then we have a perfect market.

Let us apply this to our present discussion of businesses. The man wishing to buy a business would, if the market were perfect, know exactly what businesses of the type that interested him were in the market, would know their relative advantages and disadvantages, and the prices asked for them. Similarly the vendor would know what other businesses were being offered, their characteristics and prices, and what buyers were paying for businesses of different types.

It will be readily understood that while in theory there may be a perfect market, such a situation does not exist in practice so far as shops are concerned. The buyer cannot possibly know, for example, whether other businesses have been sold at the very moment when he might be discussing one particular business with a vendor. Again, the attractiveness of a business can vary in a matter of a few days owing to changing circumstances. In fact, it is evident that, as regards retail businesses, *the perfect market, which implies full and up-to-date knowledge on the side of both vendor and purchaser, just does not exist in practice.*

It should be made clear that the nearer the market is to being a perfect market, the less is the chance of "freak" prices. If we consider a case where a buyer had not compared, with other businesses of a similar type, the business he was buying, we see that the market for him would be very imperfect as his knowledge was so limited. A seller, on the other hand, not knowing what price was being obtained for businesses such as his own, would, unless he were particularly fortunate, find it extremely difficult to obtain the current market price.

We can conclude by saying that the more the market approaches the idea of a perfect market, the more prices for businesses offering closely similar financial and non-financial attractions will tend to correspond. Ignorance, however, can produce most unusual selling and buying arrangements.

Footnote
If the living accommodation on the premises enables the purchaser of a shop to live more cheaply than in similar accommodation away from the business the difference could be regarded as an addition to the profit and therefore be taken into reckoning when assessing the goodwill.

A thorough check should be made on the advantages and disadvantages, financial and non-financial, of living on the premises. Make allowance for the cost in time, money, strain and stress, of travelling between home and shop and for the benefit of being able to get away for a break from the shop.

Whether the accommodation is part of rented or of freehold premises it will be necessary to work out what proportion of the total cost in rent (or rent equivalent), rates, insurance, etc., is attributable to the living accommodation and what is to be charged against the business.

In some circumstances it could be more expensive to live on the premises than away from them and the living accommodation might be more profitably applied to business use or sublet if this is possible and permitted. For example, it might pay someone taking highly rented premises with living accommodation in a city centre to sublet this accommodation at a substantial commercial rent and live out of town.

Consultation with your accountant and your solicitor is advised.

YOUR NOTES:-

Chapter 10

COMPETITION, PROFIT AND GOODWILL

The expectation of the future maintenance of past profits must be influenced by competition. Competition is to be considered from two aspects, that of the present and that of possible future opposition. It would be difficult to give too much importance to weighing up the competition that exists against a business you intend to purchase. Learn all you can of competitors' past effects on the business, estimate as closely as possible their future influence. The better you check on these matters, the more closely you can assess the goodwill.

Well established opposition is normally preferable to competition of recent origin, as it can more readily be gauged; furthermore, its effects are already reflected in the trading figures of the business under consideration. A recent addition to the competition influencing the business you investigate can make the future most uncertain; as uncertainty grows, goodwill decreases.

Many buyers are anxious to purchase a shop with no near direct opposition, but this can be a dangerous aim. If a business is lightly opposed there may be varied reasons. The shop may be particularly efficient and popular and so frighten away competition; it may be that so far no one has seen an existing chance to compete *and* also had the means to set up business; thirdly, there may not exist additional potential sales in the area.

A very prosperous business with little opposition can be an invitation to an enterprising man to try and break into the market. Opposition may not be deterred by the standing of the original business; indeed, such a prosperous shop is likely only to attract either the most powerful and dangerous competition or the most foolish adventurer.

From the long-term point of view therefore it is suggested that you should generally prefer the business where reasonable competition is already well established and where the relative position of the existing shops is such as to discourage any but the most foolhardy of newcomers. An obvious exception could be a business occupying a guaranteed monopoly position, such as sometimes happens on a new estate, where only one trader of a particular type might be allowed in a given district.

It is not out of place here again to remind ourselves that all goods and services compete for our money. When considering competition we should therefore take into account not only shops of the same trade as the business under review, but also competitive departments of other businesses and, so far as this can be ascertained, the general spending pattern in the district.

We have in a previous chapter suggested that the review of an area should include taking note of the number of television aerials, cars and so forth. In some districts large numbers of these goods can mean a well-to-do population with abundant purchasing power at their command; in other districts many of these cars and television sets may be absorbing, by rental or gradual payment arrangements, a large amount of the spending power of the district. *The chemist's most powerful competitor may well be not another chemist half a mile away, but the television dealer in his own block of shops.*

We suggest that the *facts behind the obvious prosperity or otherwise of a district should be examined,* just as we try to look at the facts behind the bare figures of the accounts for a business we study.

Chapter 11

SECURITY OF TENURE, PROFIT AND GOODWILL

The seller (vendor) of a business sometimes tries to obtain payment for the lease, over and above the price of the goodwill, on the grounds that the rent is unusually low for the type of shop.

The lease position obviously influences the goodwill figure, and other things being equal, the longer the lease and the less onerous its terms, the higher the goodwill. *But,* rent is one of the expenses taken into account before net profit and pure profit figures are arrived at, and therefore the low rent will *already* have had the effect of increasing the goodwill. The vendor should remember that the lease is necessary for the buyer of a business to have security and for continued profits to be earned, i.e., for there to be "goodwill".

If the lease is sold apart from the business (this being closed down or changed to a different trade), the vendor must consider what loss might be involved in sacrificing goodwill and in accepting the lower price normally obtained for stock and fixtures sold other than as part of a "going concern". In short, in any but the most exceptional cases, the value of the lease is part of the goodwill and cannot be added to it as a separate value. Sometimes a lease can become so valuable that it pays the tenant to sell to a different trade, sacrifice his business goodwill and sell off his stock and fixtures at a reduced figure. Expert advice should be sought before taking such a step.

If the vendor owns the freehold, and no rent has entered into the accounts in the past, the purchaser must, when he calculates the pure profit, allow for future rent if he is taking a lease or for interest on the capital involved in the purchase of the freehold. If an exceptionally high figure is offered for the freehold alone, the business not being required by the person making the offer, full thought should again be given to the points we have mentioned.

Although in general security of tenure is necessary for there to be goodwill value this is not always so. If the goodwill depends on a trading name and reputation rather than on a particular trading site it could mean that goodwill would not be reduced or would be only partly reduced if the shop were removed elsewhere. It is even possible that in new premises the trading name could produce more profit and the shop have more potential than in the original position.

Chapter 12
APPLYING OUR IDEAS

(to be read with Chapter 15)

The first step is to arrive at a pure profit figure, on the lines we have previously described. Later a specimen set of accounts will be studied and it may be helpful to read Chapter 15 in conjunction with this one and with the balance sheet supplement.

A

Having reached a pure profit figure for the business under review, we should compare this figure with goodwill values which are actually being obtained in the current market. We should work out the relationship between the annual pure profit and the sum paid for goodwill, in various businesses of the particular trade with which we are concerned. We may find for example that in some cases the goodwill being obtained is three times the annual pure profit, in other cases the goodwill may be one year's pure profit. We should now place the individual business we are examining somewhere in the goodwill scale between one and three times a year's pure profit, by taking into account all the factors giving rise to goodwill, as previously described, and giving due thought to the "social" amenities.

For example, a business with good living accommodation, with a rising trend of profit, and a long lease, in a desirable area, would tend to rate for goodwill in our example at three times a year's pure profit; one without accommodation, with fluctuating returns, in a less attractive district, would tend towards the lower end of goodwill at one year's pure profit. There may be occasions where goodwill is less or more than the limits mentioned, and these exceptional cases are the subject of a brief chapter which follows. *The relationships we have given above are merely examples. Actual relationships between pure profit and goodwill must be ascertained at the time of one's investigation;* they vary considerably both with general economic conditions and with the special conditions of any type of business.

As far as possible we should base our judgment on prices actually paid in the current market, as distinct sometimes from "asking prices" (the "asking price" is the price the seller asks for his business). If difficulty is found in obtaining the information, a study should be made of prices asked for businesses of the category in which you are interested, and these prices should normally be treated as maximum ones. It will be clearly seen that a vendor does not usually obtain more than his asking price and often has to accept less.

Some businesses fall outside any normal procedure and can be dealt with only on their individual peculiarities. As we have indicated earlier, the assessment of goodwill must be a mixture of art and science, of calculation and business judgment. A large measure of judgment is involved in being able to detect the business which lies outside the normal method; this is where experience counts. If a buyer lacks the necessary judgment and experience, and cannot consult someone possessing them then he might be best advised to confine himself to the orthodox straightforward business, avoiding the unusual. By so doing he might lose great opportunities of profit but he will also reduce the risk of speculative loss. *Every business transaction has its element of risk and a buyer should decide how big a risk is involved and how far he is prepared and able to gamble.*

By careful study of the trade in which you are interested you will probably be able to acquire the judgment and experience referred to above. If you are not able or prepared to do so then you should seek someone reliable who will advise you. There are agents who specialise in giving service to would-be buyers and sellers of shops. They can give valuable guidance but you should also try to develop within yourself at least the basis of a sound decision as this will help you to benefit from advice obtained.

It will readily be seen that the application of our method of assessing goodwill may be described in essence as a *comparative method*. What we are trying to do is to obtain sufficient knowledge of what is generally on offer and the prices obtaining, and of the individual business we are interested in, to decide what is a fair market price for the goodwill. *In view of the great variety of circumstances influencing the attractiveness or otherwise of any shop, it seems clear that, as stated at the beginning of this book, there can be no formula for goodwill.*

Many examples could be given of the traps found in trying to say, for example, that goodwill is a definite number of times the net profit, as is sometimes suggested. Suppose, for example, we are told that in a particular trade goodwill is three times net profit. First of all we have the problem that net profit may or may not reflect truly the profitability of a shop. Without knowing how the net profit has been arrived at, how much, if anything, the owner has paid himself before computing the net profit, and so forth, we are working on completely unstable grounds from the outset. Even if the net profit figure is a true indication, difficulties still arise.

Consider two businesses, each with an average net profit of £10,000 for the last three years. In one case the net profits might have been £9,000, £10,000, £11,000 for the three years and in the other case £11,000, £10,000, and £9,000 again for these years. In either case the average net profit over the three years is £10,000 but would you be prepared to say that the goodwill value of the business with the declining profit is the same as for the business with the growing profit? The answer is obvious, and this extreme case is used to draw attention vividly to the fallacy of rule-of-thumb formulae.

Another obvious case would be one where two businesses again showed similar net profit figures, and possibly similar pure profit figures; in one case, however, new opposition has recently opened nearby, which must affect the prospect of past profits being maintained in the future, and must therefore influence goodwill.

Finally, how can any formula take into account varying lengths of leases, availability or lack of living accommodation, attractiveness of a locality, and all the host of other factors influencing the market value of a business?

We conclude that our method is aptly described as the comparative method and this seems logical because all values are relative, all prices a reflection of these comparative values. There is no valid reason why goodwill should be an exception to this market law and hence a comparative method is soundly based.

Each buyer must decide for himself which factors influencing goodwill are most important in his own special case. The man who sets great store by security of tenure will discount more the goodwill of a business with a short lease, than will a man not so concerned with long tenure. Others may be more pre-occupied with competition or social amenities. The goodwill value of a business can vary for different buyers, according to what each of them most wants in a shop.

B

Another way to apply the pure profit figure in goodwill valuation is by what I will call the "yield" method.

Here we check on the percentage return on total capital invested made by as many as possible examples of shops similar in location, turnover, etc., to the one we are assessing. If this return averages say 20 per cent (this figure is for example only), we would decree that our maximum figure for the business under consideration should be five times the pure profit. This figure would be a *total* one for lease/goodwill, stock, fixtures, etc. If a freehold property is involved, this needs special attention.

Return on business capital reflects profits, and profits depend on markets. So both the "comparative" and the "yield" methods come back to supply and demand. These influences are not constant, and profit percentages and goodwill therefore fluctuate.

In the "comparative" method we arrive at a figure for lease and goodwill and then add the value of stock and fixtures to reach a total. In the "yield" method we arrive at a total figure *including* stock and fixtures.

In the "yield" method, if stock and fixtures are high in value, the goodwill of even a very profitable business can be heavily depressed and possibly *negative*. Conversely, the goodwill can be grossly inflated if the stock and fixtures are worth little.

Rigid use of a "formula" would offend good business sense. Here is just one example:
Think of a business with a turnover of say £100,000–£150,000, a stock of say £25,000 and fixtures and fittings of say £10,000. If we assume a pure profit of £10,000 and stipulate a 20 per cent return on capital, we would set a

maximum total price of £50,000. With stock, fixtures and fittings at £35,000, we therefore allot £15,000 to goodwill, that is one-and-a half times one year's pure profit.

In the example given, if the stock in that business had been £35,000 and fixtures and fittings £15,000, a price of £50,000 would include *nothing* for goodwill; with a stock of £10,000 and fixtures and fittings of £5,000, goodwill would come to £35,000. The return on capital in each case would still be 20 per cent, as stipulated.

Under the "comparative" method, exceptional values (high or low) for stock and fixtures would be dealt with as special issues. Clearly, a problem of high-value stock is not usually so grave for a buyer as is an over-payment for goodwill. Stock can normally be reduced even if this means cutting the price. But is an over-payment for goodwill retrievable? Only if *another* buyer, disregarding or lacking market knowledge, can be found.

C

A third method of arriving at a reasonable price for a shop is to work out what percentage the total price (for lease/goodwill, stock, fixtures and fittings etc., but NOT including the price of a freehold if this is being sold), is of the turnover for a large number of shops in the trade which interests you. Then see how any individual shop shows up by comparison.

It is important to take a large sample, say several dozen, of shops of about the same turnover and type as the one under examination, since there can be a great deal of variation in size of stock and in the value of fixtures and fittings etc. between different shops in the same trade. Variations tend to balance out over a large sample.

The broad tendency is for the price of high turnover shops to be a larger percentage of turnover than is the case for smaller businesses. Percentage profitability frequently grows with turnover as, among other reasons, fixed costs fall as a percentage and bulk buying can increase gross margins. However there are disadvantages of size as well as advantages and many small shops show a higher profit percentage than the larger ones. It is recommended that you do not rely solely on method C.

Important footnote

When using method B the pure profit calculation to be employed is different from that referred to earlier under method A. Under method B we are comparing the return on higher risk investments in shops with one another and with lower risk investments in for example building societies. For method B we therefore allow for a management salary as in method A but do NOT also deduct the return which could be received by investing in a "safe" investment the total cost of buying the shop we are investigating. If we deducted both a management salary *and* interest on the total capital before comparing yields our comparison would not be a true one.

CONCLUSIONS

A wise approach is to use all the methods described and compare results. Always we must remember that we cannot set an exact value in advance on goodwill; we are not weighing a pound or a kilo of sugar or of potatoes. And each method is at base comparative; in one case we compare the profitability of various businesses, in another the profit/investment proportion in one business with that in other businesses, and in the third turnover and prices. Elsewhere in this book we refer to the topics of return on capital, and to the economic concepts of choice and of alternatives.

Chapter 13
UNUSUAL CASES

Final proof of the goodwill value of any business is what it fetches in the current market. If a particular buyer pays, as he sometimes may, substantially more than the price as it would be assessed by the normal methods, then that is the true goodwill value. On the other hand, a seller sometimes parts with his business at a figure much below the value which expert opinion would suggest.

These extraordinary goodwill prices spring mainly from three sources; one reason is lack of knowledge on the part of buyer or seller, another is the existen e of some peculiar relation of supply and demand affecting one buyer and one seller, the third is some unusual quality of the business.

Examples of abnormal supply and demand conditions may arise from some special feature of the business or some particular desire of a purchaser, or a combination of these factors.

A vendor may own the one business of its type in, shall we say, a small island off our coast; the market for such businesses is comparatively limited, and the goodwill expected may be accordingly low. Suppose, however, we find someone who has always longed, for some personal reason, to live on the very island concerned; he may realise the vendor's small market, but he is also aware that if he loses his present chance he may wait indefinitely for another. Here we have a psychological situation which may throw up a purchase and sale agreement on quite unforeseeable terms.

Or we may have a village with perhaps the chemist's shop where a potential buyer served his apprenticeship. The would-be purchaser, at last able to consider buying his own business, has always wished to own this shop, which now happens to come on the market. Again we have the scene set for a bargain in which sentiment may predominate; who could say what goodwill value should apply in this situation? If the business fetched twice the goodwill which expert judgment and market knowledge would expect, we can only agree, despite the experts, that this was the market value at the time. **One purchaser can disprove our most finely-calculated figures. So we must avoid being dogmatic and must avoid any formula.**

Such examples can be multiplied, but should not be allowed to upset our sense of proportion. While instances of the type we refer to should not, we stress, be allowed to influence us unduly, they should do at any rate two useful things. They should warn us against being over dogmatic or over precise in our estimates, and they should make us watchful for unusual properties which can affect the selling price of our shop. Most businesses do not have some over-riding appeal to a particular buyer; it is wiser for a vendor to be satisfied with a fair market price than for him to dream that some buyer will come along to pay a figure beyond the most optimistic goodwill assessment. Purchasers should similarly not rely on finding philanthropy in the vendor.

Ignorance of the market by seller or buyer, or both, may also produce unusual bargains; both should therefore try to obtain current facts of prices at which businesses have actually changed hands. It should be of some comfort to prospective buyers that usually we find they obtain just about what they pay for; to obtain a so-called bargain often means acceptance of some disadvantage which repels the average buyer.

It can happen that a business proves almost unsaleable, even with nothing asked for goodwill. The vendor may therefore be faced with the prospect of closing down the shop and of obtaining what he can for stock and fixtures, fittings, etc. Here we may in passing point out that stock is usually heavily discounted by someone buying it other than as part of a going concern. Fixtures, fittings, etc., are in such circumstances almost always even more severely discounted than stock.

A business showing little if any pure profit, and hence in theory having no goodwill, may yet warrant the interest of a competitor. If the latter feels that by buying the shop in question and closing it down he can transfer at any rate some of the trade to his own shop, he should carefully assess the gains and losses which might result. The important point to bear in mind is that the buyer might obtain additional turnover with very little increase in his overheads. In other words a particularly profitable addition could be made to his takings.

Let us consider a concrete example: a business for sale and having a turnover of say £80,000 per annum, showing, at 30 per cent gross profit, no pure profit to the vendor. A buyer able to transfer £50,000 per annum of the turnover to his present business could add £15,000 per annum (30 per cent of £50,000) to his net profit if handling the extra turnover did not involve him in any additional overheads. While in practice the annual amount added to his profit would almost certainly be less than £15,000 he would probably find that, after allowing for any additional expense, the £50,000 added turnover transferred from the closed-down shop was at a more profitable rate than his present turnover.

The reason for the remarks we have made is that "fixed" overheads (on which a note is given at the end of this chapter) would not be changed due to the new trade; some overheads might rise, but taking everything into account it would very often be found as stated that the net profit on the *additional* trade would be higher in relation to turnover than was previously the case for the buyer's business. Another factor is that the larger buying quantities made possible might well result in increased gross profit margins.

The buyer of a business in such circumstances would naturally take into his reckonings the cost of moving stock, the legal expenses and so on, and he would need to make a careful check of the amount of trade he could hope to transfer to his own business. Based on these figures he might well find that a small shop with normally no goodwill value might have nevertheless a value to himself alone.

As a wise business man, the prospective buyer of a nearby competitor's shop should also consider his position if someone else did eventually buy the business which is for sale and perhaps introduce keener and more efficient competition than hitherto. He should assess the effect on his own pure profit of *losing* some turnover, and should balance the risks and cost of not buying-out the shop which is for sale, against the risks and cost of buying.

Fixed overheads are those business expenses which do not, over a short period, increase with a rise in turnover or decrease with a fall in trade (obviously over a long period all overheads can vary). Important examples of fixed overheads are rent and rates; while they do vary, particularly rates, they are expenses which are fixed in the sense that they must be paid whether the business is doing well or badly.

Variable overheads or expenses are those which can vary with the amount of trade being done. Examples are wages, although there is often a time lag before falling turnover leads to staff reduction, or conversely before rising turnover makes additional staff necessary. Insurance of stock and the cost of having it valued, bear a relation to the amount of stock and this amount usually varies to some extent with sales. In most businesses it is found that the proportion of stock to sales falls with rising turnover, as a basic stock must usually be held however small the amount of business being achieved.

It is instructive to divide the expenses of any business into "fixed" and "variable', and those which fall between the two. It will be seen that once a shop has earned enough to pay the fixed overheads, then the net profit on additional turnover is a higher percentage than hitherto. In other words once the fixed overheads have been covered, net profit approaches gross profit more closely.

The point we have just made draws special attention to the importance of considering the effect on any business of a fall in turnover. It is usually the *last* few thousands or ten thousands of pounds of turnover which are especially profitable: a fall of say 10 per cent in turnover can therefore often mean much more than 10 per cent loss of net profit. A simple illustration of this follows:

	A 10% drop in turnover	B 20% drop in turnover
Turnover £200,000	Turnover £180,000	Turnover £160,000
Gross profit £60,000	Gross profit £54,000	Gross profit £48,000
Net profit £30,000 (£60,000-£30,000)	Net profit £25,500 (£54,000-£28.500)	Net profit £21,000 (£48,000-£27,000)
Expenses £30,000 (fixed £15,000 variable £15,000)	Expenses £28,500 (fixed £15,000 variable £13,500)	Expenses £27,000 (fixed £15,000 variable £12,000)

(A) (10% drop in turnover)
Net profit has fallen from £30,000 to £25,500 = £4,500

$$\frac{4,500}{30,000} = 15\% \text{ drop in net profit}$$

(B) (20% drop in turnover)
Net profit has fallen from £30,000 to £21,000 = £9,000

$$\frac{9,000}{30,000} = 30\% \text{ drop in net profit}$$

N.B. Fixed expenses have remained constant while variable expenses have been reduced by the same percentage as the turnover.

The figures given are quite arbitrary, and definite practical examples should be worked out. Obviously it is a great advantage to have *fixed* overheads as low as possible. We should, of course, keep a close watch on *all* overheads.

The other side of the picture should be considered when it is felt there is potential to increase turnover. Added turnover might result in a higher percentage gross and net profit and could therefore be particularly valuable.

Calculations of the likely effects on profit of various percentage increases in turnover should be made: the comments in chapter 20 are important in this connection.

YOUR NOTES:-

Chapter 14

A VARIETY OF POINTS

The following are a few miscellaneous topics which can arise in connection with valuing a business. The remarks we make are brief but the points are important.

In certain cases difficulty may be found in selling a business even for the value of stock and fixtures; and we can therefore ask whether in some instances the goodwill value is actually negative. The practical answer to this question is "yes". For reasons which may be simple or involved we may find businesses changing hands for a price less than the valuation of stock and fixtures, etc.

A very short lease, with perhaps heavy dilapidations to be faced (to restore the property to the condition stated in the lease) may influence the seller to give away his fixtures and fittings and part of the value of his stock, in order to induce a buyer to take over these commitments. Again, a shop may have been earning consistently less than its owner could have made as an employee, and a buyer might have to resign himself to reducing his own living standards for a period during which such a neglected shop has to be built up. The conclusion is that if the price paid for a business is less than the value of its tangible assets, then the "goodwill" has fetched less than nothing. To give a simple case, if a business with fixtures and fittings worth £5,000 and stock worth £10,000 changes hands for, shall we say, £12,000, then in fact the "goodwill" has realised *minus* £3,000.

Previous reference has been made to fixed and variable overheads and it will quite readily have been seen that once the fixed overheads have been met in any business, then the net and gross profits on additional turnover will tend to come closer together. This is to say that after fixed overheads have been paid, further turnover will be more profitable than that already obtained. For example, take a business with a turnover of £200,000 per annum, a gross margin of 25 per cent and a net profit of 10 per cent, with fixed and variable overheads each 7½ per cent of the present turnover. If the turnover is increased by £20,000 per annum the additional gross profit is £5,000; variable overheads are 7½ per cent of the new turnover, i.e. 7½ per cent of £220,000, which is £16,500; fixed overheads remain at 7½ per cent of £200,000 which is £15,000. Thus the additional net profit from the additional £20,000 turnover is £5,000 minus 7½ per cent of £20,000 (or £5,000 minus £1,500) this being £3,500.

So, from the previous paragraph we see that £20,000 extra turnover has brought in £3,500 extra net profit, and the percentage net profit on the £220,000 turnover is £23,500 over £220,000 which equals 10.68 per cent approximately as against 10 per cent on the original £200,000. This increase in the percentage net profit implies an increase in the pure profit, while the gross profit has remained constant at 25 per cent. The net profit has increased by 17.5% (i.e. from £20,000 to £23,500).

A further point which should be borne in mind is that we have stated that our gross profit has remained constant at 25 per cent, while the turnover has increased from £200,000 to £220,000 per annum; but in many cases a bigger turnover can, as we have said elsewhere, mean buying on better terms and result in a higher percentage gross profit.

The implications of the above should be carefully worked out. When considering the purchase of any shop you should, we suggest, calculate the effect on net and pure profit of (a) an increase of say 10 per cent in turnover, and (b) a fall of the same percentage; reference should be made again to Chapter 13. A marginal business is one in which a relatively small fall in turnover can mean that the pure profit might be wiped out; in other words the "marginal" business is one which is hovering on the fringe of having, or not having, any goodwill value. *It is most important to bear in mind that in many businesses the last few thousand pounds of the turnover produce the significant worth-while profit.*

From the foregoing remarks we would broadly conclude that the goodwill value of a business with adequate returns well covering the fixed overheads, will normally be higher than that of a vulnerable shop where a fairly small drop in takings can seriously affect the net and pure profits. We should beware of high fixed costs and should seek flexibility in overheads; flexible overheads are those which could be reduced if business declined and which are more or less in direct relation to the turnover.

To remind ourselves of the dangers of general statements, we should mention that some flexible overheads might wisely be *increased* if trade has declined. For example a drop in turnover might suggest we should spend more on redecorating, display, advertising, and perhaps on window lighting.

Time can have an important effect on the price obtained for a shop. A vendor who must sell quickly may find it necessary to accept a lower offer than if he were in no hurry. Similarly the buyer pressed for time and anxious to buy may pay more than he who can wait. In short, time is a strong market influence.

YOUR NOTES:-

Chapter 15

A SPECIMEN SET OF ACCOUNTS: RATIOS, ETC.

We now give a typical simple Profit and Loss Account for a retail business. The layout of shop accounts varies, but the basic principles and type of information normally agree with our specimen. The essentials are the opening and closing stock figures for the trading period, which is usually (but not always) a year, the purchases and sales, and the expenditure. Our example is not intended to include every expense which a business can have, but the items given are typical.

With the following accounts before us we will then proceed, in question form, to discuss various items in them:

PROFIT AND LOSS ACCOUNT FOR THE YEAR ENDED........................

A. What stock we have started with and have since bought.			B. What we have taken in money and still have as stock.		
A. Opening Stock (at cost)	£10,000		B. Sales (at retail price)	£150,000	
Purchases (at cost)	£120,000		Closing Stock (at cost)	£12,000	
Gross Profit (B-A)	£32,000				
	£162,000			£162,000	
Rent	£3,000		Gross Profit Brought down		£32,000
Rates and Insurance	£1,500				
Salaries, National Insurance and Wages	£12,000		[N.B. From this all our running expenses (NOT capital expenses) as detailed opposite, are deducted in order to arrive at the net profit]		
Heating and Lighting	1,000				
Professional services (Accountancy, stock valuation)	350				
Postages, etc.,	200				
Telephone	400				
Cleaning	400				
Advertising	250				
Stationery	100				£32,000
Repairs and renewals	500				
Bank interest	750				
Depreciation	750				
		£21,200			
*Net Profit (what is left after paying our running expenses)	£10,800				
	£32,000				

*this is *before* taxation.

Questions and Comments

(1) Could any of the items of expenditure be reduced? Are any of them unlikely to recur? Would any of them not necessarily be incurred by the purchaser? e.g., bank interest on an overdraft should be added back to the net profit.

(2) Are any of the items likely to change in the foreseeable future? e.g., is an increase in rent or rates due shortly? This will obviously lessen the prospect of maintaining the profit level shown on the accounts. Conversely if the rates are to be reduced then the future profitability of the business is likely to be higher than that shown in the past accounts.

(3) What return, if any, has the owner had by way of salary and wages? Was any such return equal to the average salary of a manager in such a business? This is a most important point in arriving at the pure profit as described in a previous chapter. If the salaries of £12,000 include payment to the owner of an average manager's salary in this type of business, then the net profit shown is in effect a "pure profit" (after allowance has been made for interest on capital as referred to previously and after "adjusting" the figure as suggested by other questions in this summary). In short, to ascertain the pure profit we must know what, if any, payments to the owner are included in the salaries and wages shown.

(4) After the net profit figure has been adjusted in the light of these notes, how does the figure compare with the earnings of a manager in such a shop? This question is linked up with question (3) and if in fact the owner has drawn the equivalent of a manager's salary, then the pure profit can be arrived at by simply allowing for interest on capital and for other items of expenditure which do not reflect the true profitability of the business.

(5) Is the stock figure unduly high or low for the type of business, the stock figure being considered in relation to the turnover? A general check can be made by reference to published statistics, but stocks vary considerably from one shop to another according to individual circumstances; specialist advice is recommended if you do not possess expert knowledge of the trade. By increasing the capital investment required, and thus reducing the number of people able to purchase the shop, an abnormally high stock would usually detract from goodwill.

(6) How does the gross profit as a percentage of sales compare with the trade in general? Any wide variation should be carefully investigated first of all with the vendor and then with independent advisers.

(7) What is the trend of the accounts for the past three years? Two businesses may, as we have said in a previous chapter, show *identical average profits* on sales, from *opposite* trends. You should beware of falling returns unless you have definite knowledge of the cause and are confident you can overcome it. A declining turnover might enable you to buy a business at a low price, but remember you are then in effect gambling on the prospect of revival.

(8) Are you keeping in mind that goodwill cannot be assessed to within a few pounds? There is no formula, no precise mathematical answer to the question of what goodwill is worth; goodwill valuation is art and science combined.

(9) Has the vendor been receiving unpaid help from, say, family? If so, you need to deduct from the net profit, and therefore from the pure profit, what such services would cost you if you were running the business. Conversely the number of staff and their wages may be larger than if you were in control. Here an addition could justifiably be made to the net profit figure shown, provided you were quite convinced that there was definite over-staffing.

The net profit figure as shown on the accounts may therefore not directly help you as to the profitability of the business. Net profit figures *alone* clearly mean very little to us, and we must analyse the facts in the accounts and arrive at an *adjusted net profit figure* and then at a *pure profit*.

Many prospective buyers of businesses are bemused by the net profit figures shown on accounts; they may for this reason, *unless they look beyond the figures,* turn down a business which would suit them admirably or buy one which is unsuitable. There is a lesson in this for both buyer and seller. You should realise the significance of gross profit as being the sum from which all outgoings are to be made, and the study of these outgoings and of the gross profit is much more revealing than a mere acceptance of a bald net profit figure.

We should make quite clear what the difference is between the profit and loss account and the balance sheet. The profit and loss account shows what has happened *over a period of time* (usually a year), the incomings and outgoings and the resulting profit or loss. The balance sheet tells us what the business owes and what is owing to it, what are its assets and its liabilities *at the date* of the balance sheet. Thus a profit and loss account could be (say) *for the year ended* 30th September, 19____, and the corresponding balance sheet would be *as at* 30th September, 19____.

Ratios, etc.

Your attention has already been drawn to the need to study the gross profit percentage. This is clearly basic and essential; from the gross profit percentage and turnover you see how much money is available to meet all the overheads, and what surplus, if any, is left as net profit. But I suggest you go further.

Work out some other significant ratios from the accounts and balance sheets. The understanding and interpretation of these documents is a highly specialised study in itself, but you could at least do the following:

(1) If the turnover is divided into sections, for example (a) confectionery. (b) tobacco, (c) newspapers, etc., work out the percentage of each for the latest few years and note any trend. Is the least (or most) profitable section, for example, growing or falling compared with the others? Does the turnover include VAT?

(2) What percentage of the turnover is paid out on wages and salaries and how has this percentage varied over the last few years?

(3) What percentage of the turnover goes in rent and rates? Again note the trend over the years.

(4) What is the ratio between the average stock held (at cost price) and the turnover (at cost price, i.e. selling price less gross profit)? Or, both stock and sales could be at retail prices, i.e. prices to the public, which would give the same result. Do not fall into the trap of dividing sales at retail prices by stock at cost price.

The usual way of deciding the average stock held is to add the opening and closing stock figures together and divide by two. This is often only very approximate and it can be highly misleading in businesses where stock holdings fluctuate a great deal over the year.

(5) Work out the sales per square foot or metre
    (a)   of floor space in the selling area and
    (b)   of total floor space in the premises.

Always take a tape-measure when investigating a business; a camera is also useful. And, of course, you will have a notebook and perhaps a handy tape recorder.

You could usefully go further still. Measure up the individual sales areas for each main section of the business and calculate the sales per square foot or metre for each *group* of merchandise.

This kind of research could give you ideas about potential in the form of space which is at present sterile from a selling point of view.

(6) (a)   Add up the "variable" overheads and see what percentage as a *total* they are of turnover for each of the last few years.
     (b)   Total the "fixed" overheads and note their percentage.

If these percentages are growing, while the percentage gross profit is stationary or declining, what are the prospects? Could you, if you bought the business, do anything about these trends?

(7) (a)   Work out the percentage return on the *capital* investment involved in buying any shop. Please refer back to chapter 4.
     (b)   Work out the "pure" profit as a percentage of *turnover*.

(8) Study the assets and liabilities. Who valued the assets, when and on what basis? For example, has the stock been independently and professionally valued? For a gross profit figure for any period to be reliable there must be accurate opening and closing stock figures and accurate figures for turnover and purchases.

You could profitably work out many other ratios, for instance that between "fixed" capital (for example property, fixtures/fittings, etc.) and "liquid" capital (for example shares, stock in trade, etc.). The more readily an asset can be changed into money the more liquid it is. Money itself is liquid capital.

As a minimum you should find it rewarding to carry out the calculations I have recommended. Having done this you should compare the results with data given in the trade press, in any interfirm comparison documents you can gain access to, in official statistics, etc.

Try and find out the reason for any variations; be alive to *trends* and not just to *averages*.

An average over a few years might appear normal and satisfactory but a trend up or down might be a warning or an encouragement. Always ask yourself – "What happens if this trend or tendency continues?"

Chapter 16
FOR THE SELLER

The buyer of any business wishes to obtain it for the lowest possible price. Three main assets are usually being bought, with the possible addition of a fourth in the form of potential. However, the three assets are normally (1) stock, (2) fixtures and fittings, etc., and (3) goodwill. Of these, stock can be valued factually and very accurately with usually only a very small (if any) difference of opinion between experts. Fixtures and fittings, etc., again are tangible and assessable largely on a scientific basis, but with more scope for variation in expert opinion than in the case of stock. Goodwill is a subject on which many divergent views are held and it is frequently the asset which a purchaser regards as most open to bargaining.

The vendor of a business naturally seeks the highest obtainable goodwill figure. Like the buyer, he must usually take his price for stock and fixtures as fairly well fixed by external arrangement. Again therefore, like the buyer, the vendor finds usually in the goodwill element the greatest scope for his bargaining.

Thus with buyers seeking to lower and sellers seeking to raise goodwill values, a balance is reached according to the prevailing market conditions. Someone in touch with the market can, within fair limits, state what the current goodwill of a business is worth.

Where the interests of buyer and seller coincide is in their seeking a maximum pure profit. The greater the pure profit, the greater the price the vendor can reasonably ask, and the more worth-while it is for the purchaser to acquire the business. At the time of negotiation a purchaser often tries to depreciate the pure profit and goodwill, but this approach can, if carried to extremes, lose him a business of first-class earning power.

The vendor should therefore study the points about a business which will make it appeal to a buyer. Both seller and buyer should analyse the business, the former so that he can be realistic in his asking price, the latter to ensure he gets value for money according to levels prevailing in the current market. The vendor should aim at having all relevant facts available in convenient form.

Timing is of great importance. If a vendor knows that other businesses of his own type are being offered, he may be wise to defer the attempt to sell his shop. Buyers are often apt to become unduly wary if several businesses are offered in a locality at the same time, even though all the shops for sale are sound.

If you wish to sell a business you are advised to read right through this book and to make a careful note of anything you can do to help a prospective buyer make up his mind quickly.

It is to the seller's advantage, as well as to the benefit of any potential buyer, to see that all required information is readily to hand in an easily understood clear form.

Legal penalties could follow any attempt at deception or concealment. Quite apart, however, from legal and moral aspects, it is bad business to waste your and prospective buyers' time. Straightforward methods save time.

Here are some essentials for the wise seller

(Naturally what you offer at any interview will vary with the circumstances).

(1) Have on hand copies of the latest three or more years' results or of all accounts and balance sheets if the business has been running less than three years. Be able to explain as far as you can, any unusual features such as exceptionally high or low wages, gross profit, etc.

(2) Produce information on sales, expenses etc., for any interval between the end of the last financial year covered by accounts, and the time of investigation. Buyers like up-to-date information.

(3) Documents relating to and enlarging on the accounts and balance sheets should be available. For example, stock valuation certificates and any valuations of freehold, lease/goodwill, fixtures/fittings, etc. which have been carried out.

(4) Do you know how your rent compares with others in your area and with rents for new premises? A copy of the lease should be available together with details of any work such as decoration, re-wiring, rot proofing, central heating, insulation, etc. which has been done.

(5) Have by you a copy of any survey of the property.

(6) Have readily accessible information about planning and development scheduled or proposed for the area.

(7) Local maps and guide books should be in your possession.

(8) General information on social factors and amenities, schooling, recreation and so forth, is helpful.

(9) Information about staff, their qualifications, training and so on, should be of key interest to prospective buyers.

(10) Keep a note of unusual matters – for example, you might not wish to part with certain items of fixtures and fittings. Make sure this is clarified; the printed particulars prepared by your agent should do this.

(11) Your reason for selling is usually something about which an enquirer is understandably curious.

(12) Decide in advance how far if at all you are prepared to bargain on price and on any other point such as leaving over part of the money, reducing stock, etc. Realise that we cannot reasonably be dogmatic about goodwill values.

(13) Information about competition and competitors should be available for discussion.

(14) Decide in advance whether you *want to* [and if so whether you *could*] assist a buyer in financing his purchase. Would *your* bank help? – this would be an excellent recommendation for the business. Your bank would probably be keen to retain the business account which they might be in danger of losing to a new owner's bank. Would you like to keep a financial interest?

CAUTION

Make sure any information you give orally, in writing, or in any form, is correct and can be verified. Distinguish very carefully between what you are giving as a fact, and what you are giving as an opinion in good faith; be cautious about any data which can vary over time.

Use judgment. Try to detect the time waster. Have a word with your agent. He might know whether someone coming to see your business is likely to be serious or not. This is one of the most useful advantages of engaging an agent to sell your business. But try to be patient with the *suspected* trifler; yours might be the chosen business.

Make it clear to a potential buyer that any special "on the spot" arrangement is subject to approval by your solicitor and other advisors.

Do not be upset if a prospective buyer wants to check what you tell him. Encourage this.

While your honesty and frankness might sometimes appear to have lost you a buyer, this is in fact unlikely. People investing in a shop are I observe becoming better informed; they tend to grow more and more knowledgeable, less and less gullible. So good business and good moral behaviour should coincide. And your agent can feel more confident in sending prospective buyers to you if he knows you will be fair as well as ready with information on hand. Give the "fors" and "againsts" and this will engender confidence in those who visit you.

It could pay you to take independent advice from a business consultant about the potential of your shop, whether and how it could be improved, the cost, and the likely return on any investment. Such a report, if favourable, might be a strong bargaining aid when dealing with a prospective buyer. An unfavourable report might (a) help you to be more realistic in your views on the value of the business, and (b) influence you to postpone selling until the business is a better buy for someone, until it could justifiably win you a higher price.

Try to look at things both from the would-be purchaser's viewpoint and from your own. You are aiming to sell so you must consider what motivates the buyer.

Be cautious about giving people "first refusal" or an "option". If you must do this set a time limit. *Consult your agent* before giving any such undertaking.

Have you decided how you will use or invest the proceeds of the sale and on your overall plans for the future? Commercial and non-commercial factors are linked together.

TIMING

Try to decide well ahead about when you wish to sell. You can then make a calm rational approach to the move, you can plan to have all the required data available, you can, as you have time to spare, pick the best time to offer the business.

If you are under pressure to sell quickly you can be in a much weaker bargaining position than if you are not rushed.

With wise advance planning you might be able to say to your agent "I shall want to sell during say the next two or three years; let me know when in your opinion the time is most opportune". Markets can fluctuate rapidly; do all you can to time your operations with adequate current market knowledge. Here again your specialist agent can be of immense service.

Perhaps your business has certain disadvantages you cannot remove. You are not usually able, for instance, to alter its trading position or to make the neighbourhood more attractive. Do not however accept too readily that you cannot improve the selling chances.

Seek out the points in favour of the proposition, with the assistance of your agent. Think of the disadvantages your business does not have as well as those present and hard to overcome or reduce.

Tell a prospective buyer frankly and fairly what you sincerely believe could improve the business and explain why you have not done these improvements. Maybe you are short of capital, or your health is bad, or you want to retire. Perhaps you just lack the motivation!

A prospective buyer of your business might or might not be well furnished with facts on gross margins, etc. in the trade concerned. In any event, you, as seller, would be sensible to have information at hand; details from any interfirm comparison in which you take part could be particularly useful here.

To summarize. Put yourself as far as you can in the situation of a prospective buyer of your shop. How would you like to be dealt with if you were buying?

Chapter 17

STOCK

The basis on which stock is valued for business sale purposes is normally that of *current market cost price*. The buyer must usually be prepared to pay whatever the goods in the condition, variety, and quantity in which they exist on the day he takes over, would have cost him to buy in the usual way from wholesaler or manufacturer, at that time.

There may be certain cases in which vendor and purchaser agree on a price between themselves, but in most instances an independent valuation is both necessary and desirable. It is difficult for any seller to avoid bias in assessing the value and saleability of goods he has himself bought. It is against human nature to admit a mistake, and this seems particularly true over mistakes in buying goods. As to the buyer, he is obviously keen to avoid payment for anything he considers unsaleable or in any way doubtful.

The ruling principle in the absence of any special arrangement is that only good, clean, saleable stock should be included at full current cost price in the valuation; any items not within this description, that is, not clean *and* good *and* saleable should be suitably discounted or not taken as being of any value at all. Any goods treated as of no value are the property of the vendor and he should remove them if he so wishes.

In considering the saleability of stocks which are clean and good, we must look at them in relation to the business being sold. A buyer should not be expected to take over at full cost price, goods which are grossly in excess of normal requirements for the business. The vendor is in the best position to state what is, for his business, an average normal stock of a particular item, but here it is most difficult to avoid bias. The purchaser will presumably have, at any rate, some general knowledge of the type of merchandise he is buying and of the amounts usually held in stock by businesses of the type involved.

The buyer should not aim at too great precision so long as the merchandise is clean and good, but he will be prudent to consider the general balance and size of the stock in its relation to the overall price for the business. In other words, stock size and condition influence goodwill.

Any gross over-stocking or serious unbalance of stock would tend to depreciate a goodwill figure. (Certain exceptional circumstances are referred to later in this chapter.) In extreme cases a highly excessive stock could reduce the goodwill obtainable to a figure much below the one otherwise to be expected; such a stock may occasionally even render a business quite unsaleable.

This topic of stock size and balance is one where precise guidance is not easy, but the buyer should seek information from the vendor, draw on his own experience, check on trade statistics (as for example Board of Trade figures) and obtain advice from an impartial expert. The term "clean" as applied to stock is self-explanatory, while the description "good" implies that the article so described is, so far as can be checked, in accordance with any legal, trade, and customary standards which apply.

The question of stock valuation is so complex and offers so many possible sources of dispute, that the wisest plan is to appoint independent valuers and leave the matter in their hands. Such valuers may act for both parties, the contract stating that their valuation shall be final and binding, or each party may have his own valuer, provision being made for a referee should the valuers disagree. Once a valuation has been carried out as laid down in the contract, no discussion of the prices placed on individual items should be permitted, as this can lead to prolonged controversy and can invalidate the valuation itself. The valuers would, unless there were any contrary clause in the contract, take at full current cost price only stock which is good *and* clean *and* saleable; they would reject as valueless or suitably discount any stock not falling within this description.

We should emphasise once more that opinion must enter into the valuation of most stocks. The views of buyer and seller are likely to diverge and it is therefore, we stress, advantageous to bring in an independent valuer, one who is a specialist in the trade concerned.

Earlier in this chapter we mentioned certain exceptional circumstances relating to the size of stocks. In times when goods are scarce, what would normally be termed over-stocking may in fact be good business. In such a case a buyer may well find it necessary to pay a higher goodwill figure than otherwise just because large stocks of scarce goods are available; this, it will be seen, is the reverse picture of the pruning of a goodwill figure which over-stocking usually implies. On a falling market, large stocks would be even more severely scrutinised than normally, and small ones could favourably influence goodwill value. When we write of large or small stocks we mean in relation to turnover.

The special circumstances we have just referred to are perhaps a little outside the scope of this book, but they should be kept in mind. The general principle is that the larger the stock in relation to sales, the greater the risk involved in buying it. But here, as in so many cases, the prevailing market conditions must be the guide.

A vendor, faced by a purchaser with barely enough capital, might offer to co-operate by reducing stock before the business changes hands. In such circumstances the purchaser should make sure, as far as he can, that a stock reduction is not going to curtail service and have adverse effects on the goodwill. Secondly, the purchaser should be quite clear how the stock is to be reduced and be careful lest the quickest selling part of the stock bears the brunt of the reduction, leaving a smaller stock but one with a higher proportion of slow moving lines; this could mean that the purchaser would soon need to find the very capital he lacks, the shortage of which has forced him to seek a stock reduction on purchase. Thirdly, if an agreement is reached that only a certain value of stock is to be taken over by the purchaser, then it must be clearly defined how a decision is to be reached, when the valuation is completed, as to which stock is excluded from the transaction.

Until the valuation is completed it will not be known whether the stock is above the amount the purchaser has contracted to buy.

It will be seen that an undertaking by a vendor to reduce stock, or an agreement that only a certain value of stock should be bought, can cause many difficulties; it is most important that a clear understanding be reached at a very early stage in the negotiations.

It is sometimes said that any stock reduction arrangement is unworkable and almost bound to lead to dispute. This is rather an extreme view and much depends on the extent of mutual trust between the parties and on whether they will "give and take".

In some cases a purchaser might agree to take all the good clean saleable stock provided the vendor would accept delayed payment for any amount over an agreed maximum. Or a percentage discount on the amount to be paid for any stock over such a maximum could be negotiated. Arrangements must be clear and included in the contract.

Chapter 18
FIXTURES, FITTINGS AND RELATED ITEMS

Almost every shop has, in addition to stock, some means of storing and displaying goods, and often tools and apparatus used in work carried on as part of the business. There are normally also items useful to the customers; from mats to weighing machines, from chairs to umbrella stands; then there will be files, reference books and so on used by the retailer.

All the items we have mentioned in the last paragraph, and many more, essential in greater or less degree to conduct of the business, are included in the general term "fixtures, fittings and trade utensils". The border line between fixtures and fittings is not always clear and for our present purpose the distinction is not necessary. What is important to the purchaser of a business is whether any given item falls somewhere within the general group dealt with in this chapter, or whether an article would be excluded from the group in a valuation. The custom of the trade concerned must be a guide and should be interpreted in any particular case by professional valuers, if possible by *specialist* valuers.

We must stress the importance of finding out whether any of the articles we are discussing are the property of the landlord, or on hire purchase, or for some other reason are not owned by the vendor of the shop.

In a chemist's business, the professional apparatus such as dispensing measures, dispensing balance and so forth would be classed under "trade utensils". The customary wall cases with their glass fronts, drawers and cupboards, the front counter, the cash register, the familiar personal weighing machine, would rank as fixtures and fittings. All the foregoing items would be included in a valuation of fixtures, fittings and trade utensils for purposes of transfer of the business.

71

Difficulty can arise with shop fronts and windows. Usually the shop front itself is not included in the group we are discussing and a buyer of the business does not normally pay for it directly, as it is an essential part of the shop landlord's property, and not an addition; similarly the plate glass window is not included in a valuation. The window back, however, the base of the window and, of course, the display aids such as glass shelves and supporting rods and so on are included in any valuation.

A purchaser should ensure, if he is not already familiar with the custom of the trade in which he is buying a shop, that he has the necessary knowledge of what he is paying for. He is well advised to confess any doubts to a skilled valuer and to rely on the service of such an expert.

The valuation of fixtures, fittings and trade utensils is a blend of knowledge and judgment. Market knowledge is the key and there is no simple formula available for valuing such items. A purchaser of a business should, if he is not himself expert, acquire at any rate a general knowledge of values by everyday observation. Many items such as chairs and electric fires are common to business use and domestic life; a buyer should study prices in catalogues and trade journals, visit an auction sale occasionally and so on; he should study prices asked for fixtures, fittings and trade utensils in all businesses he investigates.

Equipped with this general knowledge, the prospective buyer will have at least a rough means of judging the reasonableness or otherwise of the price asked for the fixtures, fittings and trade utensils of a business. If the total figure is obviously not excessive he may decide to accept it without having an independent valuation, but if he is in any doubt he should call in an expert.

There are certain general principles to be observed when assessing items of the type under discussion. The following are some of the factors to consider:

(1) The age and condition of the items (bear in mind the occasional instance where age may add to value rather than detract from it). Age usually reduces value but the condition and suitability for purpose must be considered.

(2) The quality of construction and material.

(3) The suitability of the items to the shop. Fixtures and fittings are sometimes quite out of keeping with the business. They may be too elaborate and high-class or below the standard for the type of shop. In either case their value would be less relatively than it would be in appropriate surroundings, and a buyer may find it necessary to dispose of either type before the end of their normal period of usefulness. In short, their value partly depends on the shop in which they are placed. We should remember also that the items covered by this chapter are usually severely discounted in value if disposed of other than as part of a business sold as a going concern – see (5) ahead.

(4) The necessity of having any items in the business concerned. This is linked up with (3) above, but requires separate attention. A buyer may find items of equipment, perhaps expensive ones, which are in the business, appropriate, *but little if at all used*. Such articles should be dealt with during preliminary negotiations and a clear understanding reached in writing as to whether or not the purchaser is buying them and on what basis if he is doing so.

(5) The buyer should bear in mind the difference in value of *the same items* when they are (a) *in situ* (literally "in place") that is in position as part of a going concern, and (b) when they are being sold apart from the business. The *in situ* value is usually much higher and the buyer of a going concern should expect to pay this price*. It is not generally justifiable for him to expect to buy part of a going concern's assets at the price applicable to a separate sale of assets. The fact that the purchaser may wish to scrap all the fixtures and fittings and to refit is not decisive in this connection, as the business has been doing the volume of trade on which the goodwill is based, with the use of the fixtures and fittings there at the time. Usually therefore the purchaser of a going concern should, as stated, be prepared to pay the *in situ* value, although the price placed on fixtures and fittings will, of course, influence his view of the goodwill value of the business.

(6) The purchaser should ascertain, we repeat, whether any items seen by him in the business are not the property of the vendor. We have especially in mind high value goods such as cash registers and neon signs, computers, etc.

---

*In some cases the value could be much higher *outside* the business; for example, there might be rare articles used in the business to give "atmosphere" or for decoration.

(7) Clear arrangements should be made at an early stage about any items which the buyer cannot use; an example is a facia board which might be of considerable value, but which bears a name not in future applicable to the business.

(8) A written inventory of the fixtures, fittings and trade utensils included in the transaction should be prepared and attached to the contract of sale. It should be made out even if they are not being valued at the time.

(9) Any items excluded by the vendor from the sale.

SPECIAL NOTE

Sometimes an *inclusive* amount is asked for lease/goodwill, fixtures, fittings, etc.

It can be very important from a taxation angle *how* the amount is divided between (a) lease/goodwill and (b) fixtures, fittings, etc. A division will have to be made at some stage.

The interests of Vendor and Purchaser might be opposed to one another. Do *not* make any private arrangement. Do consult your accountant.

Chapter 19

ACTION CHECK: SUMMING UP SO FAR:
FINDING THE MONEY

We have now reached a definite stage. We have defined goodwill, and analysed the factors on which it depends; we have suggested a basis for assessment. Our examination so far has included our ideas on how accounts should be studied and has shown that figures by themselves can be a dangerous guide. We have considered stock, fixtures and fittings, etc., in relation to the price of a shop.

Anyone proposing to buy a business and acting on the principles outlined in this book can feel he has been thorough to a degree for which few have sufficient patience, skill and insight. *Some people may lack the time and freedom to follow all our suggestions, but these should be pursued as far as is possible.*

Having outlined an ideal, which perhaps not everyone can carry out, we shall now suggest an absolute *minimum* scale of enquiry into a retail business. We shall pick out various points from previous chapters, add to them and state what *must* be done by any purchaser to check up sensibly on the shop he proposes to buy. Ask yourself the questions we list, and record *in writing* the answers you make:– space has been left for this.

(a)　　How much money have I available?

(i)　　　Of my own,

(ii)   From other sources. What are the terms on which outside money is available? Will the lender also want to investigate the business and if so will this cause delay and possible loss of a suitable chance? Is the money available without doubt when required?

(b)   If I borrow, how much will this absorb of the income from the business and for how long? What happens if the venture fails? Consider capital repayments and interest and the advantages and disadvantages of a limited company. *N.B. Remember that capital repayments have to be made out of income on which tax has already been paid if applicable, although tax relief might be obtained on interest payments. CHECK AT THE TIME WITH YOUR ACCOUNTANT.*

(c)   Exactly what type of business am I seeking; what conditions must it satisfy as to:

        (i)   Location,

        (ii)   Living accommodation,

(iii)   Schooling,

(iv)   Income produced,

(v)   Family needs, etc., if applicable. Have I fully consulted wife or husband and children or other interested parties; are all agreed on which kind of business is to be bought?

(d)   *Have I made my own scale of choices? For example, is money the main factor, or how far do I sacrifice income to social and other amenities?*

(e)   Am I qualified technically, temperamentally, and socially, to conduct the business I propose to buy? Here it is essential to be realistic and to take the advice of a candid friend.

(f)   Can I live on the income expected from the business? Have I allowed for the expense involved in buying, removing and so on?

(g)   Have I investigated the area,

(i)   In general?

(ii)   Specifically in the immediate district of the business?

(iii)   By walking round the district, and if so, for how long and over what area?

(iv)   How many times have I visited the locality and shop, on what days and at which times? What were the weather conditions?

(v)   Have I made a rough map or maps showing barriers to trade, competitors, open spaces, transport, shopping routes, and so on?

(See Chapter 25 on the value of maps.)

(vi)   Are local development plans going to affect the area; have I checked with local authorities?

(h)   Have I fully checked accounts; does my accountant approve?

(i)   How many shops have I previously investigated; if none, what expert advice have I had?

(j)   Have I studied the broad economic basis of the area and the special points relating to the immediate surroundings?

(k)   Have I checked the condition of the property, my obligations under any lease, and have I had a surveyor's report?

It will do no harm to repeat that our basic aim is to assess goodwill by calculating the degree of likelihood that existing custom will continue. Here we should stress that we must distinguish between *goodwill* and *potential;* the importance of this will become more apparent when we turn later to considerations of potential.

And now a word of caution and encouragement. It is important not to go to extremes: both over-investigation and under-investigation are dangers to be avoided. We can find reasons to stop us buying any business, however good, as readily as we can take the easy way of looking over a few figures and glancing at a shop and district.

Some men and women are so careful that no business has a hope of passing their scrutiny, while on the other hand at least one man has been known to buy a shop without being aware of opposition in his own trade a mere one hundred yards away. This book aims at helping a purchaser to find the happy medium, to know what he is truly seeking and to make as few errors as possible. The complete avoidance of any errors is not possible.

Let us face squarely the fact that the ideal business does not exist. Always you have to accept some aspects you would prefer to see altered; you will not obtain just the position *and* the accommodation *and* the rent *and* the other benefits you desire. Something must be sacrificed, but you should make sure that it is not one of the basic requirements. In listing these requirements *on paper* rather than mentally, decide which are essential and which could be given up if necessary. As we have said before, to know what you want adds precision to your search and helps you avoid loss of an opportunity.

Remember the seller is not necessarily waiting for your decision alone. Do not expect him to refuse others while you perhaps lose him weeks of selling time. The good investigator is usually prompt and quick, with much of the ground-work done in advance. Many would-be buyers have been furnished with details of a business, had copy accounts, gone away and carefully checked matters for weeks, only to find at the end of their examination that someone else has already acted.

Remember too that goodwill is not a matter for an equation. *Judgment and experience can be as vital as figures.* The market finally decides, and often the seller's opinion is in the end proved right on the matter of goodwill. He too will study the market and may not agree with the buyer's views. So if a business suits you, do not haggle too closely over a few pounds, as not even the expert should be dogmatic on a goodwill valuation. You should try to avoid treating as purely scientific what we have previously described as a mixture of art and science. *You should be more concerned with what you can earn from a business if you buy it than with what has been done in the past.* What your predecessor earned is history which does not always repeat itself and the information should be looked upon as a very valuable guide indeed, but not as a guarantee. *Your* expenses and profit will have to come from *your* results.

FINDING THE MONEY

Here are some ideas to consider:-

(1) *Look at your own resources:* e.g. properties, insurance policies, shares, etc.

These might be used (a) directly or (b) as security for a loan. Decide whether it is wiser to (a) sell the assets or to (b) raise a loan and employ them as security.

You will have to consider interest rates, your tax position, the current market for selling assets, etc. Expert advice should be sought at the time, as conditions can change and the whole matter is individual. Such points as your age, health, commitments, etc., influence what is possible and what you will decide.

(2) *A bank loan.* Discuss with your bank manager and accountant the points for and against a fixed loan and a floating overdraft.

(3) *Insurance Companies.* You might be able to use a Life Policy for a loan; the Company would not normally want the policy to lapse.

(4) *Friends and Relatives.* Remember you should still have written formal arrangements approved by your own and the other person's solicitors.

(5) *Trade or Professional Bodies.* Loans by such bodies are often at favourable interest rates and the organizations can be in a good position to help you to investigate a business.

(6) *Finance Houses.* Remember that if you are asking a lender to take a more than usual degree of *risk* you must expect to pay above the usual interest.

(7) *The Vendor himself.* Find out whether a vendor's willingness to lend is based on his confidence in his business or on his desperate need to sell. A vendor might be both confident and desperate, or the business might be one very difficult to dispose of. Why?

If you purchase on instalments, making gradual payments to the vendor, have everything put into legal form. See that the contract is clear about who is controlling the firm while the payments are being made. Expert legal and financial advice is something you cannot risk doing without.

(8) *A Guarantee.* Here someone else is providing security for you to get a loan and they will usually expect to have some return for this.

(9) *You could advertise for a co-director or partner.* Before you do this make sure you understand the points for and against partnership and the formation of limited companies. You would be most unwise to enter into partnership with anyone about whom you do not have the fullest knowledge and about whose reliability there is any doubt. Ask your solicitors!

(10) *Agents.* Your specialist agent could well be in touch with *possible* sources of finance.

(11) *Obtain details of the services offered by Investors in Industry (3i) P.L.C.*

(12) *Wholesalers and Manufacturers in some trades might help finance your purchase.*

(13) *You might consider taking up a franchise,* of which there are numerous varieties. The basic principle in many cases is that the purchaser gets the right to use the name of an established product or service, for which of course he has to pay.

The payment made is in respect of the established goodwill of the merchandise or service and in addition there might be equipment and stock to be paid for. The buyer of the franchise normally has a guarantee against competition from another franchise holder within a certain area and very often "easy payments" can be arranged.

The buyer of a franchise is usually provided with guidance on selling methods and general business organization and management by those selling the franchise. The purchaser runs the business more or less as his own but might have to pay a percentage of his takings as commission to the vendor. You should take specialist advice before committing yourself.

(14) *Building up your own capital.* An elementary study of the principles of economics shows us that capital can only be accumulated by curtailing present consumption and putting off doing or buying some of what you would like to do or buy straight away. Many successful business men and women have found that once you have built up a very small amount of capital you can quickly multiply it if you can face continued restraint for perhaps only a few years.

From what I have said it is clear that (a) the further in advance you can decide that you want your own business and (b) the more you are prepared to make some sacrifices for the time being, *the greater can be your success once you have got over an initial period of self-denial.* And as a "bonus", apart from the actual building up of capital, you can also build up credit worthiness and confidence with your bank or other backers if you demonstrate your will and ability to save. Then you can be well placed for outside finance if needed to help still further growth.

As a very simple example of how capital can accumulate within a business, (for instance by a shop owner wishing to buy another business), let us consider a small shop where the turnover could be increased if a bigger variety of goods were kept in stock, and where the owner is at present short of capital.

Suppose the owner, for a time, keeps his own personal income from the shop to a minimum and so can put shall we say a further £100* into stock instead of drawing it out of the business. £100 will, if a net return of 10 per cent is made on it and if it is turned over (as stock) and reinvested in stock eight times in a year, grow to $£110^8$ in this one year, that is to just over £214.

At the end of the year the sum of £214 approximately is available for further expansion and if reinvested as before can more than double itself in the next year. This process of reinvestment in the business can help a small concern to grow rapidly into a large one *provided the market is there and the necessary self-restraint.* By the sacrifice, for example, of one short holiday, the capital of a shop can be substantially and quickly increased.

* I have used £100 merely as a convenient unit to illustrate the point.

GENERAL REMARKS

You might well have further ideas of your own on how to find money. The basic financial question you must answer is:- "Can I start or buy a business with my own resources or would I have to raise the money elsewhere?". Then ask:- "Am I wiser to borrow money now, if I can, or should I build up my own capital and then buy?". Or "Should I borrow some of my requirements and build up the remainder by my own efforts?"

To answer these questions you will need to know whether in fact you are able to borrow money and if so on what basis the interest is to be calculated. You must be quite certain of what the true rate of interest is; for example is the interest calculated on the reducing amount of the loan or is it a fixed percentage of the initial amount borrowed?

You will be sensible to take independent professional advice on interest rates, on the terms generally of any loan, and on your individual tax position.

It is essential that you define fully, in writing, and in collaboration with anyone else involved, your aims and objectives in buying or starting a business. You should have a realistic budget control plan, simple or full according to your needs, and you should prepare or have prepared for you a D.C.F. (Discounted Cash Flow) analysis of the proposed investment.

In the midst of all these calculations, remember that you will be wise to think on the relationship between business and non-business motives.

Make sure that you protect, as far as is economic and possible, by insurances, etc., both yourself and anyone dependent on you.

Be aware that if you, as a director of a limited company, give a personal guarantee for any loan to the business, you will lose the protection of limited liability. Before giving any such guarantee go fully into the matter with your accountant and make sure you know where you stand.

Financial assistance might be available to you through various government schemes and you are recommended to check on the up-to-date position regarding grants, the Business Start-up Scheme, etc. Study also the information issued by the banks and others on borrowing for business purposes, on factoring, on leasing equipment, and on government guaranteed loans.

Chapter 20
POTENTIAL: THE NEW BUSINESS

The difference between goodwill and potential is not simply a contrast between past results and future hopes. The distinction to be made is between the likelihood that past results will continue in the future, and the chances of future expansion. In short, if we buy goodwill we pay for the probability that past results will be maintained. If we buy potential we buy the possibility of doing more in the future than has been done in the past.

In our investigation of the foundations of goodwill we have examined the various factors which have produced past results. Our suggested procedure and method of assessing goodwill has been based on considering pure profit and its sources and also social factors. We have tried to find out how to weigh up the chance that past returns would be maintained in the future; the factors influencing this prospect will naturally also affect the hope of increase in profit, that is the potential.

New considerations, as well as the factors which arose in connection with goodwill, are involved in assessing potential. It will be clearly seen, for example, that an increase of population combined with proposed new building plans in a certain area will have more effect on potential than on goodwill as we have defined it. Again, proposed *new* transport facilities will be a factor in potential.

We should turn once more to the factors giving rise to goodwill – position, amenities and so forth. We should re-examine all these factors, together with trends of population in the area, building plans and so on, from the critical viewpoint of whether they indicate scope for definite *increase of profit in the future* as distinct from *maintenance only of past results*.

We can clarify the matter by taking, as we shall shortly, the case of a newly opening business. A new shop must start without goodwill* as we have defined it in this book as there are no *past* results to assess; all that such a new

---

* But of course an already well-known and respected business or individual starting a new shop would have the advantage of the reputation and name of their already established business(es).

business can possess is potential. *The growth of a successful business is a process of constantly transforming potential into goodwill,* that is, of turning hopes into performance. The market and other investigations we should make before opening a new shop include those we should carry out in valuing goodwill; but the assessment of the money value, if any, of potential, presents even more problems of judgment. *Many of the comments we shall make are very much opinion, and we shall offer ideas and suggestions rather than firm conclusions. This must be so because with potential we are considering something even less tangible than is goodwill.*

Very often the purchaser of an established business refuses to pay for potential; he claims that any potential will result in profit only through his own efforts and he sees no logic in paying for the opportunity to work hard. Against this, however, one would expect to pay more for a business with obvious room for expansion than for a shop with similar past profits but without the potential. As we have already indicated, it is more complex to assess potential, which is largely a matter of judgment and imagination, than it is to evaluate goodwill based on pure profit as shown by carefully interpreted figures and on other factors.

It would seem therefore a fair initial statement to say that *generally* the value if any to be placed on a *potential* pure profit of a given sum per annum would not be so high as the value placed on a similar annual pure profit already achieved in the past. The question of a newly opening shop must be given special attention and, as already stated, will be referred to later in this chapter.

The potential of an *established* business may be of two kinds; one of them is that already present when a purchaser takes over, while the other is potential which will become available in the future.

Some examples of the first type are scope or potential due, say, to the inefficiency, the illness, the defective personality, the lack of capital of the vendor. This may be regarded as dormant potential, as an opportunity to benefit from *already existing circumstances which the vendor has not exploited.*

A few examples of the second type are the proposed building of a new block of flats near the shop, the extension of transport to reach a shopping parade previously poorly served in this way, the planning of a new arterial road which may prevent many in the neighbourhood from going to patronise a nearby rival. *This form of opportunity offers new markets to be explored;* it is in marked contrast with the more intensive cultivation of markets which are already there.

The purchaser must decide which of the two broad forms of potential is more valuable to *him,* and which he is more suited and able to take advantage of. The two types could both be available in the same business, for example the vendor may have been ill and there may also be new building planned nearby.

1. We first consider a business that is showing no pure profit, i.e., one producing not more than the return a manager of such a business could obtain for his services and on the capital needed to purchase the shop in question.

(a) We should ascertain the price which each of several businesses of the type referred to has recently fetched *above the value of the stock and fixtures.* The difference between the total price and the value of stock and fixtures is what has been paid for potential (assuming no payment is made for social amenities) and we should calculate what relation this excess bears to the annual "adjusted" net profit (average for the latest three years) in each case (see chapter 15). We compare prices with net profits, as no pure profit is being made.

Let us assume that the prices (above the value of stock and fixtures) received for three businesses of the type under discussion are £2,000, £4,000 and £6,000 and that the annual "adjusted" net profits were £12,000, £16,000 and £20,000 respectively. Then the potential may be said to have realised on the average:

$$\frac{£2,000 + £4,000 + £6,000}{£12,000 + £16,000 + £20,000} = \frac{£12,000}{£48,000} \text{ or } \frac{1}{4} \text{ of a year's net profit.}$$

We would probably be justified therefore in judging the value of the potential of a similar business under consideration for purchase, as being about ¼ of a year's net profit. The result of ¼ is, of course, only an example; the figure will vary according to circumstances.

This method we have outlined is based on a comparison of known and unknown and is put forward only for use in the case of established businesses not making a pure profit. We have assumed that no payment is being made for social amenities; in some cases, however, pleasant accommodation or attractive location commands a price in its own right.

(b) An alternative approach could be that described later in this chapter when we consider the newly opening shop. We could estimate the potential pure profit which might be made in the future from the business at present showing no pure profit, and could then proceed on the broad lines described (under section 2) for the new shop.

What we have done so far is to say that normally a business with no pure profit will, in the absence of social amenities, only sell for more than the value of the tangible assets if the purchaser believes that potential exists. We repeat that in method *(a)* we have related the payment for potential to the *net* profit, as there is no *pure* profit with which to compare it.

2. We now turn to the case of a *newly opening business*. Perhaps the prospective owner is offered empty premises on rental, either with or without a premium for entry.

Rent and any premium should, for our present purpose, be converted into an annual rent equivalent. For example, a rent of £1,000 per annum for 14 years plus a premium of £2,000 down will be equivalent to an annual rent over the 14 years *not* of £1,000 per annum plus £2,000 divided by 14, which would equal £1,140 approximately per annum, but of considerably *more than* £1,140 per annum. The reason for this is that £2,000 premium is paid in advance and one must take into account the interest this could otherwise earn for the purchaser over the period of the lease, add this to £2,000 and then divide the total by 14 before adding the £1,000 rent. The interest should be calculated as compound, not simple, interest. Please refer to Chapter 29 re D.C.F.

The first investigation to be made is of the potential market for the goods and services to be offered. In some cases the rent asked is so high that the experience of the prospective buyer can then at once show that the proposition would be uneconomic for his type of shop; no time need therefore be wasted on further investigation.

If on the face of it there seems to exist the possibility of successfully opening, careful research should be made on the general lines described previously when we discussed the investigation of an existing business. When a *cautious* estimate of likely sales has been formed, the approximate average annual pure profit likely to be made for the first three years should be worked out. This pure profit is calculated in the way described previously, by taking into account expected sales and gross profit and deducting from the gross profit the expected overheads, an owner-manager's salary and interest on capital. Some of the figures used must perforce be approximate only and any bias should be towards over-rating rather than under-rating expenses. If there is found to be no pure profit based on the rent and any premium asked, then it would seem fair that no premium is justified; the investigator might, in fact, seriously question whether the venture is worthwhile.

Should a pure profit be shown as the result of our forecast the following procedure can be adopted. First of all ascertain the average number of years' or fraction of a year's pure profit being at present obtained for *goodwill* by the vendors of established businesses similar to the proposed new shop.

Suppose this ratio of goodwill divided by average pure profit is 2½ in the case of the established business. Then we can say that unless there are most unusual circumstances any premium or charge for potential in a new shop should not be as high as 2½ times the anticipated annual pure profit; in other words we have established an upper limit. Earlier in this chapter we had argued that, in relation to pure profit the price to be paid for potential should not be as high as the price for goodwill. The risk element in estimating the potential of a shop not yet opened is obviously greater than that in assessing the goodwill of an already established shop; this justifies the view that a lower *relative* figure should be paid for such potential.

We should not be dogmatic on the point we are at present discussing, but it is suggested that normally the factor of potential in relation to expected pure profit should be substantially less than *(perhaps not more than half of)* the factor for goodwill in relation to *achieved* pure profit. Potential can be worth something, but only in rare cases is it worth as much as goodwill based on equal pure profit. There will always be the exceptional case where the potential warrants a high price; to be able to detect such a case can mean great profit.

We have dealt with the business which is being newly opened and with the "no pure profit" established business. We shall now try to decide whether in fact we can separate goodwill and potential in the case of an established business with a pure profit.

3. *(a)* In the case of an established business with a pure profit, we should first assess the goodwill on the lines previously discussed, i.e., on the basis of x times the annual pure profit; we should then examine most critically any claim that potential exists. Only concrete facts as referred to previously, are to be admitted, for example, so many new houses or flats with so many new potential *customers,* as distinct from mere *residents.* We should weigh up the prospective addition to sales, conservatively, and thus the addition which could be expected to the pure profit, after allowing for additional expenses in dealing with the increased trade. This *additional expected pure profit should then be multiplied by a factor to decide on the market value of the potential.*

As already indicated, no hard and fast rule can be given as to the factor by which the additional expected pure profit should be multiplied; it seems clear that it should be less normally than the multiplier used in calculating the goodwill of the business. In the writer's opinion a buyer should look most closely before making any payment for potential in an established business; practical experience supports this view.

We should always remember that any business tends to lose some customers and any *new* trade obtained is partly replacing the losses which are inevitable. In short, some new custom is needed merely to prevent the decline of a business.

(b) We could try to apply the comparative method to valuing the potential of an established business with a pure profit record. This would involve deciding whether the current prices obtained for similar businesses included some payment for potential as well as for goodwill.

A strong argument could be put forward for showing that in the case of an established business with a pure profit one should attempt only to arrive at a combined price for goodwill and potential. In the case of a business to be newly opened, and also in that of an established business with no pure profit, it would seem quite justifiable to deal with potential on the basis of the suggestions in this chapter.

The subject of this chapter is fraught with difficulties, and we advise the greatest caution in paying for potential unless there is the most concrete evidence of its existence.

Anyone proposing to open a new business or to buy an established one should draw up a detailed financial budget to cover the transaction.

The budget must be in writing and must embrace all the costs and expenses, with dates for payment: it must also list, with dates, the resources you will use to meet these debts.

Once the business is yours you should, I urge, maintain a budget control system, however simple and basic this is to start with. The first step towards a budget control system is an estimate of expected sales. A reasoned estimate, based on all the information you can gather, not a mere guess.

When you are running your shop you should plan in advance, and should continuously be forecasting, with dates and in detail, money to be paid out and money to be received. Divide the transactions into *current* and *capital* items.

Many books are available on this topic of budget control. An introduction is given ahead in "Stock Control"

It is sometimes possible, especially in a new development, to negotiate a lease where the rent is linked for a period to the turnover achieved. This can be advantageous in conditions of higher than normal risk and could indicate confidence by the developer in the prospects for the trading site or that it is proving difficult to find tenants. The arrangement can be especially helpful when a shop is of the type requiring a longer than usual length of time to build up to a profitable sales volume. The tenant should be careful to guard against being penalised by the agreement if sales grow more quickly and higher than had been expected. Do not lightly accept a short-term benefit if it could mean a long-term disadvantage.

Expert analysis is needed and it must be clearly understood that we cannot normally hope for the rewards of successfully taking high risks if we are not prepared or able to undertake such risks. In short, you cannot have it both ways.

"PEOPLE FIRST IN RETAIL"

a human approach to competitive retailing

by E. A. Jensen,
B.Com., M.P.S., F.I.Pharm.M.I., M.Inst.M.

book target: To help produce more money, more enjoyment, from a shop.

Contents

I.S.B.N. 0-9502208-4-1

Ask your Bookseller, or if in any difficulty please contact the Publisher, E. A. Jensen.

Chapter 21
PREMISES, LAYOUT AND POTENTIAL

A shop can, through its available space or present layout, be severely limited in potential. With many small businesses, space and layout deficiencies are the main bars to an increase in turnover, and however efficiently existing facilities are used they must usually set a top limit to turnover, even if this limit has not yet been reached.

A buyer should consider:

(a)   whether present facilities are being used to full effect in producing pure profit; and

(b)   whether potential can be created or increased by rearrangement or replacement of fixtures, etc., by modification of structure, by adding to the premises, *or* by a combination of these steps.

Having estimated what additional revenue should be obtainable from alterations which are necessary and possible, the cost of such changes should be worked out. What we require is to know the likely additional pure profit; this potential pure profit can then be assessed on the basis given in the chapter on potential. A discounted cash flow analysis should be made.

It will be remembered that we have stressed the possible difficulty in separating goodwill and potential, but none the less an assessment of whether potential exists and of its amount, should always be made. Where there clearly is potential, we can obviously justify payment of a higher price than the goodwill alone merits. We may, as stated, not be able to say exactly what should be allocated to goodwill and what to potential, but the object is an estimate of likely future *total* pure profit whatever its source.

Where the goodwill figure for a business appears high, it may be well worthwhile to consider whether there may be potential to justify at any rate a higher price than you might otherwise agree to.

To return to the question of any modification of layout and fixtures. We should first of all find out the capital outlay involved, and also the interest which is being sacrificed in other directions if the money is spent on the business.

The outlay and interest should then be converted to an approximate annual amount over the period expected for the effective usefulness of the changes, or for the length of the lease, *whichever is the shorter*. This annual cost is to be used when forecasting the pure profit of the business, and we emphasise that the figure reached can only be approximate. What we should try to do is to set the annual cost of improvement against the additional returns to be expected from such changes.

In many cases it can quickly be seen that premises and layout do not warrant much capital outlay on rearrangement or refitting. The investigation we outline will

(1)   help you to avoid outlay on improvements which may look well but not bring in an appropriate return; and

(2)   show very often where a comparatively small outlay will result in greatly enhanced profits.

Security

Full consideration should be given to the security of premises. How vulnerable are they to fire, theft, and to other risks such as flooding, subsidence, and so on? What additional precautions would you feel obliged to take, what might you be compelled to do to the property, what could be the cost, what are the insurance implications? If the vendor has not fulfilled all legal obligations and it has not yet come to light this will not relieve *you* of the obligations.

Chapter 22
PROFIT, A FEW IDEAS

Much of this book has been built on the idea of profit as related to the market price it can command in terms of payment for goodwill. A few comments on the nature of profit do not seem out of place.

Profit may be considered as the difference between what you pay for something and the price at which you sell it. This profit, which is before taking into account the costs of selling the article, is the gross profit; when the selling costs are subtracted it becomes the net profit; by going a stage further, as previously shown, we reach the pure profit.

It is obvious that unless a gross profit is made there must be loss; unless, of course, and this does not happen in practice, no expenses of any sort are involved. On ethical grounds the making of profit has been questioned, but the writer cannot recall any suggestion that morality calls for the making of a loss. Those who criticise "profits" often appear to have little idea of net profit and still less conception of pure profit.

Most people do not seem to doubt the morality or desirability of selling goods at more than they cost, in the ordinary way of business. Again, they do not usually question the need for a shopkeeper or owner of any business to make a living out of it. What is often eyed with some suspicion is the so-called surplus or pure profit; this is what many uninformed people really think of as net profit. In effect, pure profit is the profit available after all expenses have been met including payment for the owner's services and interest on his capital.

It is sometimes felt that there is something wrong in having a surplus beyond what can be earned as a manager and beyond what the investment of capital in safe channels could bring in. In the Middle Ages much thought was given to the idea of what was called a "fair" price for anything, or a "fair" profit; the view was that profit should not be what the market would bear, but something linked up with moral ideas of equity and justice. We might ask ourselves whether similar ideas should prevail today and if so who is to say what is a "fair" profit? If profit were limited, not by competition but by law, to a certain stated amount, who would fix the amount and what would be the effect?

Our first step should perhaps be to ask what is our object in producing a pure profit and why are we prepared to buy the prospect of pure profit as we do when purchasing goodwill? Is it naive to ask why men seek money beyond payment for their services and for the use of their capital? Businessmen regard this extra return as a reward for risk-bearing and enterprise and we could ask ourselves why should such risk-bearing and enterprise warrant a special return; what, in fact, does the surplus provide for the man who obtains it? At this point we should reflect that earlier in this work we had described profit as the return to risk-bearing, wages as the return to labour, rent as the return to land, and interest as the return to capital. These are broad statements which need no elaboration here. Profit, more particularly pure profit, we can say, is justified as being necessary to promote risk-bearing. To the argument that risk-bearing is a function of doubtful value there are at least two obvious replies. These are that risks exist in business, as in all human activity, that the fact, whether palatable or otherwise, of these risks must be accepted, and that very few men accept risks without the prospect of gain. Secondly, that, dependent as we are ultimately on Nature, with its uncertainties, risk is inevitable.

We can pursue the critics of pure profit a little further. If we consider the economics of any salaried worker or wage earner, we find that he is not normally content to work for a return equal only to his expenses of living, that is a wage to cover travel, food, clothing, housing and so forth. The worker desires also to have a profit as it were, this being the excess of his total receipts over his outgoings. This profit can reflect itself in savings of all kinds, and any excess by which this profit is greater in any individual case than is normal for the type of worker concerned, is in effect a sort of pure profit. In short, the more efficient or the more fortunate worker makes a surplus comparable with that of the more efficient or more fortunate business. If such a worker changes his job his previous earning capacity normally influences the salary he can command and there is therefore an analogy with the goodwill obtained for a business. To draw a further comparison we may point out that some wage earners increase their surplus by keeping their expenses down, others by taking every chance to expand revenue in the form of earnings.

The foregoing remarks apply to labour of all kinds in a free market. Such a market is rendered inoperative or is distorted by any influence which prevents or reduces the opportunity for free individual bargaining on salary or wage between employer and employee.

In the present state of our economic knowledge and social organisation there is, it seems, nothing to be gained by attacking the making of pure profit. *If we do attack pure profit we should realise that employers and employees alike aim at making a surplus and therefore the problem should be treated as one of importance to all and not as a social sin of part only of the community.* The attempt to make a profit is not confined to any one class or branch of society.

Our present system, complex as it is, has produced much increase in welfare as this term is understood generally. Until therefore we know a little more of the real workings of the system which has been built up, are we wise to tamper on theoretical grounds with the mainspring of something which works, even if it is not perfect? Should we concern ourselves more with how we each use any surplus we have made, whether as employer or as employee, rather than with the intricacies of the ethics of making a surplus? Maybe in this sense the thinkers of the Middle Ages were right in relating economics and morals.

We have asked a number of questions in this chapter without attempting to give the answers, but these brief notes may not be thought out of place in a book which has so often referred to pure profit.

The reader is referred to *On Your Head* by E. A. Jensen.

expand your potential – private and business – in 84 days

ON YOUR HEAD (2nd edition, 1981)

by E. A. Jensen, Bachelor of Commerce, Pharmaceutical Chemist

This book offers a practical guide to achievement, with a philosophy based on personal responsibility.

It is aimed at the serious-minded, at those not to be seduced by promises of effortless wealth and happiness.

ON YOUR HEAD claims that the foundations of material and non-material success are self-knowledge, enlightened self-regard, self-acceptance expanded into self-development, clear realistic goals.

Our capabilities are vast but usually unexplored. A little time, a lot of thought, a few minutes a day for 84 days of self-discipline along simple lines described in this book, could transform an entire private and business life.

ON YOUR HEAD calls for active participation. It is not for the lazy, not for the self-satisfied. It could reward you out of all proportion to your effort, yet this effort there must be. In short, the outcome is "on your head".

Extracts:

". . . our first aim is to change ourselves, not to reform others."

"One of the messages of this book is that the picture that we have of ourselves governs our behaviour and our fate . . ."

". . . we can improve, not merely maintain, our brain work as we grow older . . ."

"We can, if we are wise and tolerant, learn more from enemies who revel in telling us of our failings than from friends who gloss over the bad while praising the good."

"A correct self-image of yourself as a driver will give you confidence and control and a constructive attitude towards yourself and other drivers."

"We shape life. We are not the passive victims of fate but the active beneficiaries of all that is placed before us."

"Your bad qualities you will deal with most effectively not by frontal attack but by cultivating the virtues which oppose the bad."

"Prayer should be an expression of constant awareness of blessings bestowed upon us, not a request for favours to be granted."

"New ideas, new activities, keep us perpetually young."

". . . we must not fool ourselves that our problems of inflation and unemployment, of violence, are *causes* to be dealt with one by one."

"The brain has mechanisms to guide us towards success and away from failure; we are built to succeed."

"Competition and my philosophy are partners, provided the competition is in harmony with the natural law I have propounded."

"Inflation, like so many problems, is at base a moral problem."

"You gain by giving."

Chapter 23
WEAKNESSES TO BEWARE OF

We can hardly repeat too often that profit is made as a result of risk successfully undertaken. Risk and goodwill must, as we have shown, always be associated, but there are some cases where the uncertainty is particularly great.

There are factors which can make the purchase of a particular business unusually hazardous, the shop being we say "vulnerable"; by this term we mean the shop is more than normally liable to a fall in profit and to a failure to produce results as favourable as in the past.

At present we are not concerned with those variations in trade and profit which are part of the everyday life of retail business. We propose to pin-point certain types of risk which must be watched most closely by a prospective buyer. Before tabulating the risks we have in mind (and you may possibly add risks which you feel might be abnormally dangerous in your own individual case), let us repeat a warning given earlier in this book.

Remember you are investigating businesses with a view to buying, not with the object of finding something to enable you to reject every shop offered. So it is suggested that you make sure that any fears that a business is especially vulnerable are based on sound facts and are not merely a sign of indecision in yourself. On this basis we will now list certain businesses which should be the subject of more than ordinary care in investigation.

(1) *The shop with no near opposition.* Absence of opposition may mean either that the shop is so strongly entrenched as to have kept rivals at a good distance or that the area can only support shops of the type concerned if they are well spaced out. The point to consider is: if there is a shortage in the area of the type of shop you are considering, would a purchaser of the business soon find that he would have new opposition to trim his profits? Unopposed

businesses can be much less desirable than those with normal known opposition; yet businesses with little competition may be the very ones which *apparently* justify a high goodwill figure.

(2) *The shop with too much opposition.* This business is more readily detected than that which is unopposed. Beware of the shop where there are so many competitors, or where the quality and power of the shop opposite is so obvious, that immense effort and good fortune will be required for your success. Check how often any shop has changed hands.

(3) *The business with a gross profit barely enough to cover overheads, these overheads including return on capital and payment to the owner of a normal management salary for his work.* In such a business a small drop in turnover and gross profit can quickly result in the removal of any pure profit and perhaps in actual loss.

When buying a business it is wise therefore to consider the effect on profit of a fall in turnover; it is useful to work out how much the gross profit could fall without causing financial difficulty.

(4) *The shop where overheads are very inflexible.* We have already discussed the question of fixed and variable overheads. The fixed overheads must be examined carefully, as these have to be met irrespective of the amount of business being done. This present heading should be read in conjunction with the previous one and calculation should be made of how much turnover could be lost without making it impossible to meet the fixed overheads.

(5) *The business depending for much of its custom on a few large customers,* loss of one or two of whom may have a very serious effect. A balance should be struck between having a very large number of small sales and a small number of large sales.

(6) *The shop relying largely on fashion trade or on a single localised industry* rather than on diverse employment of its customers.

(7) *The business with stock or fixtures and fittings, etc., which are unduly high in value and cost.*

(8) *The shop which you may consider buying because it appeals to you for unusual reasons.* (We have referred to unusual goodwill values in another chapter.) Remember you may have great difficulties in re-selling if you have bought a business of very narrow appeal.

(9) *The shop which has prospered as a result of unusually long hours or arduous conditions;* here again re-sale might be most difficult.

(10) *The shop with little security of tenure,* for example, having a short lease or involving property which is due for demolition. As the question of a short lease is of great importance, the reader is recommended to make himself familiar with the broad outlines of the protection given to a tenant by the 1954 Landlord and Tenant Act. A talk with a solicitor would be well worth while on this topic.*

(11) *The business likely to be affected by such projects as development plans for the area, the building of a new shopping centre and so forth.*

(12) *The business which is handling any price-maintained products.* Is price maintenance being enforced?

(13) *The business with a gross margin which is substantially different from that normal for the trade and for the type of shop.*

(14) *The business where audited accounts and reliable stock figures are not available.* In particular it should be remembered that unless the stock has been correctly taken year by year no reliance can be placed on the gross profit figure shown; the net profit must therefore be equally suspect and from that the pure profit.

There may be acceptable reasons given by the vendor for a gross profit lower than one would expect for the business concerned. A purchaser knowing that he himself would make a higher gross percentage need not therefore turn down a business merely because of a hitherto low gross margin.

---

* There is a mass of legislation on the relationship between landlord and tenant. You must have legal advice on the *current* position.

YOUR NOTES:-

Chapter 24
MAKING UP YOUR MIND

The points we list in this chapter are less obvious and straight-forward than might appear at first sight. The suggestions are given with a view to helping a prospective buyer to put his problem into concrete form and to overcome the stage of indecision which affects many seeking a business.

(1) *A clear definition, in advance, of the business you seek, is one of the greatest helps to making up your mind whether you have found the right thing.* Such a definition calls for a full listing of your assets in the form of cash available from your own or other sources. You should also be certain that you are in full agreement with any business or non-business associate or prospective associate. You should also remember factors which are not directly of a business nature, such, for example, as the effects of your decision on your wife or husband, family, home and so on. *You should, as a definite minimum, have a clear view of where the business is to be, what type of business you want, and how much you can pay.*

(2) *Accept the fact that you must take some business risk;* decide how much risk you can afford to take in relation to the assets at your disposal. Here again non-business factors come into the question and the young single person can often take risks which may not be warranted for the man or woman with family responsibilities.

(3) *Try not to waste time on minor points; accept the fact that you will never find all you seek in any one business.* You should therefore make sure of the essentials and be reasonably flexible on other points. A *written* note of what is considered essential, prepared jointly with other interested parties, can be a great help. Such a written record often keeps you on the correct track when you are faced with a decision on one particular business.

(4) *Spend considerable thought in advance as to the extent to which you can undertake any recurring commitment or any liability of unknown amount.* A particular source of trouble can be a guarantee to stand security for another person; such undertakings are frequently given without a full understanding of the meaning and possible consequences.

(5) Many of us waste time in taking, or trying to take, a quick decision on a matter which need not be decided immediately. When you have a problem to solve, consider how long you have to arrive at a decision and avoid a hasty judgment which you may wish to reverse later.

(6) Sometimes speed of decision is of the greatest importance and there are times when almost any decision is better than none. It has been said that no businessman is correct in as many as half of the decisions he takes, that prolonged thought is therefore a waste of time, as a guess has the same chance of being correct as has the pondered decision. Guess-work is not recommended as a policy, but we do see many people spending time deciding on minor matters where it is not greatly important which way a decision is made but it is important to save time.

(7) We should always remember that some matters are best left to resolve themselves.

(8) Not every problem has a solution which can be acceptable to all the parties concerned. It must therefore be realised that some drawbacks must always be accepted from any individual's point of view and that the impossible should not be expected. A problem should *at the outset* be analysed to see whether it is possible for it to be disposed of with unanimous agreement or whether there are basic difficulties which can only be solved by "give and take".

(9) Knowledge in advance promotes speed of decision, but we must beware of having sufficient knowledge to make us doubtful yet insufficient to give us the confidence that our decision is correct. *Knowledge without judgment and balance can breed doubt.*

(10) We are told that two heads are better than one, but very often too many heads are much worse than no advice at all. If you need advice you should find a counsellor of good repute and knowledge and then give him your confidence. All manner of people tend to think themselves qualified to give advice on retail business, and it is easy to reach a stage of confused outlook which quite prevents a rational decision.

(11) A would-be buyer of a business should always keep in mind that while he is debating matters the vendor might very well sell to somebody else. In short, do not imagine, as some prospective buyers apparently do, that the initiative rests solely with you.

(12) A useful method of deciding upon the wisdom or otherwise of a decision you have in mind is to write down fully the results of your decision. Very often the action of writing gives you a more objective view and you might very well persuade yourself that the decision you have in mind is not the right one.

(13) It is a great help to have developed a general philosophy of business and life. The more clearly you can have fixed in your own mind how much you are prepared to sacrifice for money or independence, the quicker will you be able to arrive at the basic features of any decision you are called to make.

(14) The whole process of making a decision is one of elimination. First of all the unimportant and minor points should be filtered off, as it were, and then one by one you should work from the known factors to the unknown until you are finally left with the basic choice involved.

Quick decisions can spring from sheer ignorance or from exceptional ability. Indecision often comes from lack of knowledge or partial knowledge; sometimes only enough is known to enable one to see the difficulties, and these are allowed to figure too largely in the problem. If, like most people, we are not business geniuses, we should aim at a decisiveness bred of adequate knowledge and judgment.

YOUR NOTES:-

Chapter 25
MAPS AS A HELP

It is the writer's view that maps are not sufficiently used in the investigation of retail businesses. A picture, even if only crude, of a shop in relation to its neighbourhood, is frequently much more revealing than a study of the facts without such aid.

The suggestion we wish to put forward in this chapter is that to help in your choice of a shop you should always make a map or maps, that you should show on them as much data as you can, and that you should read them in conjunction with the other information you gather.

Although we have suggested that you should show on maps as much data as you can, there is a danger in making any one map over-elaborate. It is better to use two or more maps than one which is so packed with detail as to be confusing. Clarity and simplicity in each map is the ideal, and you can, by the use of maps on transparent paper, and by placing one on top of another, compare different combinations of information.

Our basic map should be one to cover the area from which the business under investigation normally draws its customers; it should preferably reach a little beyond this area. The map will vary with the type of shop involved; at one extreme there is one for a shop enjoying a monopoly or near monopoly of one of the islands off our coast. In such a case the map may be relatively simple if the population and buying habits are stable. If on the other hand visitors form an appreciable part of the customers the map may help by showing where these visitors come from, and might suggest means of catering more efficiently for their needs. Nearness of a shop to the arrival or departure points by air or sea might be of importance. Position relative to hotels and boarding houses, and the routes most used by the visitors and residents can be brought out with great clarity on a map. A map may, for example, suggest the advantage of a kiosk or small branch to be opened perhaps only during the season of heaviest traffic, the site of a box for films to be left in, or for an automatic machine for film purchase. A map can often make the points mentioned, and many other points, much more apparent than would otherwise be the case.

As a complete contrast, consider a business in the crowded shopping centre of a large town. The turnover is perhaps almost all from the passing trade of customers brought in by bus, car or rail, with some also from offices and houses nearby. A map in such a case will need to cover at the most only a few square miles, possibly only a hundred yards or two in each direction, and it should indicate competitors, car parks, bus stops, rail and bus termini and so forth. In such a case it may nevertheless be wise to draw a larger map showing where more distant customers come from, in addition to a map giving the local population served.

We may need to portray the suburban business, either of the shopping-parade type with passing trade and residential customers, or of the category without supporting shops and relying almost wholly on the regular custom of local residents.

Yet another type is the country business which might draw on an area of one hundred square miles. Here communications with neighbouring villages or towns which either compete for trade or provide customers, are of great interest. There is the market town with its peak of business on market day, and the village which loses custom to the larger town on such days.

We have mentioned a few only of the types of business we may have to assess. Now let us consider in more detail the facts a map can bring out and the varying forms of map applicable to differing shops. We repeat that every business is unique and each map must be drawn up with a particular shop in mind. The following general principles should therefore be adapted to the individual case under examination.

First of all draw on transparent paper a map to include the main roads of the district. Mark this map to show the position of the opposition in different directions and of the main residential areas served.

A second map, also on tracing paper, should show such facilities as car parks, cinemas, post offices, etc., and could also show which are the busier sides of the roads near the shop. Observation at different times of the day and year will soon reveal the routes taken by the public from, say, car park to cinema, from railway station to large multiple shop, etc. Lines joining these pairs of factors can often be very revealing as to the best position for a shop and will sometimes show what a great difference can be made by a matter of even ten or twenty yards in a shopping centre.

A map could be prepared, again on tracing paper, to show the site of proposed new building and development. Such a map placed over the previous map of customer traffic on various roads can very well show whether existing busy spots are likely to be made busier still or to be damaged by the new development.

A map showing a shop in relation to such barriers as railway tracks, canals, parks, etc., can often show, more clearly than the usual methods of investigation, why a business is not doing the trade a casual survey might suggest. A shop on a road near a railway can be strongly affected by the distance of the nearest bridge over the railway; if badly sited, the business can fail to possess a very big part of what one would normally think to be its trading potential.

The suggestions we have made are brief and by no means complete. Simple maps of the type indicated, giving in visual form information which you feel of particular importance to the individual business you are investigating, can prove a real help in business analysis. Each map, simple in itself and, we repeat, drawn on tracing paper, can often clear up obscure problems.

Useful supplements to the type of map we have suggested are the aerial photographs available for many towns; these can be especially helpful, in the case of a growing town, to suggest the likely trend of business following new building and road development.

For someone seeking a business *in a specific area,* basic maps of population, etc., could be prepared in advance. Then any business coming on the market in the town or district required can be added to the basic map and considered in the light of information already set on paper. Here is an excellent example of the value of advance preparation and of knowing what you want and where.

YOUR NOTES:-

Chapter 26

THE "IDEAL" SHOP

This book is meant to be constructive, to help you to buy the right business, not merely to stop you buying the wrong one. The cautionary remarks we make should be read with balance, otherwise you could well find some reason to reject any business, however sound.

The views of buyers naturally differ on what they believe is the ideal or perfect business, but the features that we shall list are those on which a great number would agree.

If you are prepared to buy a shop which presents only few of the qualities named, it may mean you can obtain your wishes for a comparatively low price, through there being a general lack of demand for the particular type of business you seek. Check your views against the following properties which may contribute to the ideal shop, but remind yourself once more that in fact the ideal business does not exist. You should try to get as near as you can to perfection but should accept the fact that you will not find it. Here are the properties to look for:

(1) A substantial rising turnover, with solid prospects for further increase.

(2) Profit margins, gross, net and pure, equal to, or at any rate not below, the standard for the type of shop you seek.

(3) Pleasant location with social and business amenities.

(4) Moderate *fixed* overheads and other outgoings of reasonable size.

(5) Stock not substantially more than is normal for the type and size of business; preferably the stock should be smaller than average rather than larger, in normal conditions.

(6) Fixtures and fittings, etc., should be suitable for the business and appropriate to its character; they should certainly not be over-expensive in relation to the shop.

(7) A heavy fall in turnover, if it came, should not bring the *fixed* overheads dangerously near to the gross profit.

(8) There should be security of tenure, the lease being of reasonable length, with no adverse planning development in view.

(9) If freehold property is being bought there is normally much greater security of tenure, but in this case more capital is tied up and care should be taken that only a fair market price is paid.

(10) The price of the business should be in line with the market conditions prevailing, and should have been arrived at in the way we have described.

(11) The business should be one which would have a ready market should you need to sell. Even if you have no present intention of selling you should remember that circumstances might cause a change. Thought should be given to those who might have to sell after you are no longer interested in a business.

Our list should be added to by the reader. The points have been made very briefly, and each one should be read in relation to fuller comments made elsewhere in this book; we do not propose to go through them one by one to qualify the remarks made. The amount of stock should, for example, be considered in relation to market conditions, and when the goods in question are scarce then naturally a larger stock could be more desirable. Similar reasonable interpretation of the other points is left to the reader.

FINALLY – Please remember that no shop is perfect.

Chapter 27
WHERE TO LOOK FOR SHOPS FOR SALE: THE AGENT: THE MARKET

1. You can consult a firm of Business Valuers and Transfer Agents. These agents may deal with shops in many trades or they may specialise in one trade. *Explain fully what you are looking for and state what you can afford to spend.* You should not forget to let the agents know when you have found a suitable shop, whether it is through their introduction or not; you should also not fail to inform an agent if you have already had introduced to you a shop of which he sends you details.

2. You can reply to advertisements in local or national newspapers, or in the trade journals for the particular kind of shop you desire. There are some papers which make a special feature of "Shops for Sale". Advertisements are sometimes inserted by the seller himself, and often by agents on his behalf.

3. You may hear quite by chance of a shop for sale. A friend might, for example, tell you that some tradesman he knows is thinking of retiring or of moving to another town, and that he therefore wishes to sell.

4. You might learn through a solicitor, accountant, or bank manager, that they have a client about to sell a shop.

5. Sometimes you could know the seller and be told by him.

6. You could advertise your requirements.

7. A "For Sale" notice in a shop window might catch your eye.

It is vital for anyone buying a shop to have as much market knowledge as he can gather. This market knowledge is precisely one of the things you can obtain by consulting a Business Valuer and Transfer Agent. You are advised to approach such an agent, if possible one specialising in your chosen trade; if you peruse the trade paper you will doubtless see advertisements by agents of the type we mention.

In addition to the valuable market information they supply, agents offer many other important services to the man or woman buying a shop; these services include, for example, the valuation of stock and fixtures, etc. The advantages to a seller of placing his shop in the hands of an agent are equally obvious.

The following is adapted from an article contributed by the author to *Retail Chemist,* **to which publication acknowledgement is made:**

Do you believe that the goodwill of a business must always be worth at least what was paid for it?

How would a vendor react if told that his shop would probably fetch less for goodwill than the sum he handed over many years ago?

As with everything that has a price, the price of a shop will, under competition and in a free society, depend upon supply and demand, upon the market, *at the time of selling.*

Those who read books on economics will find many references to "perfect" and "imperfect" markets. In practice "perfect" markets do not exist, although world markets for some merchandise (cotton, chemicals, wheat, metals, for example), do approach this state.

A "perfect" market is one in which buyers and sellers are in such close and rapid contact that up-to-date information on prices, on what is being offered and demanded, is constantly available to the parties.

In these circumstances sellers cannot get more than the market price and need not take less.

Conversely, buyers cannot find "bargains" and need not pay "over the odds". This is, of course, after allowing for transport, insurance, etc., costs, where these are involved.

Markets range from the almost perfect to the highly imperfect. In the latter case, buyers and sellers are ignorant of the market conditions, or the goods of interest to them are so individual (perhaps unique), or so rarely bought and sold, that there is hardly a market in the usual sense.

What of the market for retail businesses?

This market is not perfect; shops are all different, not standard; they cannot be finely "graded" as can say cotton and wheat. BUT, sufficient are sold, and sufficient of them are sold through specialist agents, for there to be a market much less imperfect than that for many things sold.

So if you want to buy or sell a shop and you wisely want to know the market, you are prudent to enlist the services of a specialist agent. You can study the advertisements, make private enquiries, chat with friends, and so on. *Free* advice from *some* sources (where the price of the advice reflects its value), is often not lacking.

Remember that prices asked for businesses are not always prices actually obtained. The agents know the figures *paid* for the businesses they handle, and this is crucial information; it is what matters.

I emphasise: *there is no "formula" for goodwill assessment.* No one can say that the goodwill of a shop is worth a certain sum until it has fetched that amount.

However, a specialist agent is in the position of having detailed knowledge of a large number of businesses on the market and of a large number also of those people seeking a business. He can compare, he can assess and relate, supply and demand; his market knowledge and expertise enable him to advise on value, using judgment and not a so-called formula.

To draw on the specialist agent's store of market data gives a buyer or seller valuable insight into the *heart* of goodwill values, into the *current* real-life market, into *what is happening now.*

So far we have touched on only a part of what the agent offers. He also puts buyers and sellers in touch quickly and selectively; he "marries" what some want with what others have to offer; he is skilled in drawing up particulars of shops for sale, in advertising, in finding out what people want.

And – a very important point for *sellers* – he usually knows which are the serious and solid prospective buyers and which are otherwise. Lack of such knowledge can cost a "do-it-myself" seller much time, money and frustration.

In economic terms, the agent helps to make the market less imperfect. To put prospective buyer and seller in touch is a lot, but it is only a beginning.

A business does not change hands as easily as the inexperienced might imagine; the sale of *any* business can be complex.

Often the hardest phase for the agents is when the negotiations start in earnest; this is when differing viewpoints and interests of the parties tend to show themselves and have to be reconciled if at all possible. Now is the time when a *patient, skilful negotiator,* can make the difference between success and failure. Here is where the agent can keep things moving.

Buyer and seller are not the only ones who can usefully draw on the services of the specialist agent; he works closely as well with the solicitors, accountants, and other professional people concerned; he contributes his special knowledge of technical business transfer aspects peculiar to his speciality.

Here is a summary and extension (not exhaustive) of what the agent offers:

- *Market knowledge.*
- *Putting buyers and sellers in touch.*
- *Negotiation.*
- *Valuation.*
- *Technical know-how, technical knowledge.*
- *"After-service".*
- *Suggestions on sources of finance.*
- *Correspondence with other professional advisers involved.*
- *Intimate and lengthy knowledge of many shops and their history.*

Chapter 28

THINGS TO DO WHEN YOU HAVE FOUND YOUR SHOP:

A SPECIMEN CONTRACT: NOTES THEREON

When you have made your investigations and decided upon a business, there are certain steps you must take before you can bring the deal to a conclusion. Do not let these things worry you, but rely on the professional help available.

The following points are a broad general guide to normal procedure, but there will be variations according to the individual case. Further things to be done will no doubt occur to you, but do not over-complicate matters.

1. Make sure that the agent who introduced the shop to you, and your solicitor, have full details of the terms of the proposed purchase.

2. Send a deposit "SUBJECT TO CONTRACT", to the agent concerned for him to hold as "Stakeholder". This deposit should be for 10 per cent approximately of the total estimated purchase price including stock; as the exact value of the stock will not be known until after the valuation, the deposit can be only approximate. It is usual for the stock valuation to begin on the day you take over the shop, the figure being as at opening time on that day.

The term "subject to contract" means that you are not legally committed to buy, and the seller is not legally committed to sell, until a contract satisfactory to you both has been drawn up and contracts have been exchanged. Your solicitor will explain in more detail, but the important point is for you to remember the term "subject to contract" when placing the deposit.

3. See that your solicitor is told, by you, or by the agent, the name and address of the vendor's solicitor. Usually the seller's solicitor draws up a draft contract and sends this to the prospective buyer's solicitor for approval or amendment.

4. If the property is to be surveyed, this should be arranged through the agents or your solicitor, and you can find out from them what the cost will be.

5. Notify any other agents with whom you had registered your requirements, that you have found a suitable shop.

6. When the legal formalities have been completed, and a date for you to take over the shop has been fixed, there are other matters to be attended to, both business and domestic. No doubt your wife will remind you of the latter, which may range from schooling arrangements to making certain that you will have milk and bread delivered at your new address. There is no need for us to enlarge on the domestic matters, but we do suggest that a list be prepared in advance, as the thoughts occur.

7. The business matters referred to in the last paragraph will vary from shop to shop, and here again a list made out in advance will be most helpful. The following are a few general reminders only; they are not a complete summary.

(1) You should let suppliers of goods to the shop know of the change in ownership, and try to meet at least the more important ones.

(2) You should, as far as is possible, let customers know of the change. Sometimes a seller is willing to stay on for a period to introduce the new proprietor.

(3) Arrange to meet the local officers of any professional or trade body of which you are a member.

(4) The authorities for such services as the telephone, gas, electricity and so on should be notified, also the local rates office.

(5) You should see the local bank manager, your accountant, and any other professional men who can do so much to help you.

(6) If the shop is one for which certain licences are necessary, as, for example, where methylated spirit is sold, be sure to obtain a current licence in your own name.

(7) If the premises need to be registered with some governing body, and also the change in ownership, make sure this is done in good time.

(8) It is well worthwhile to make the acquaintance of the local police.

(9) You would be well advised to meet your landlord or his agent.

(10) Where appropriate, a notice could be inserted in the local papers, and the national trade papers should also be informed of the change.

(11) Make certain that the Registrar of Companies is informed if necessary.

(12) Do not forget to ensure that you arrange for the insurance concerned with stock, fixtures and so forth. Check with your solicitor as to when your responsibility starts.

(13) Carriers, road and rail, should be notified.

(14) Make suitable arrangements about any shop items which are on hire, or to which part payment or hire-purchase agreements apply.

Others points will doubtless come to your mind, in connection with the particular shop you are buying; you may also decide that some of the suggestions made do not apply in your case. *But as far as possible have ready in advance your list of things to do.*

We can now look at a specimen contract of the type often used in the sale/purchase of a shop.

N.B.1 You are advised to employ a solicitor in connection with any agreement to buy or sell a shop. The specimen contract is to give you a *general idea only* of what is involved. You require your solicitor's guidance on the form and contents applicable to your *particular* transaction.

N.B.2 A contract is, broadly, an agreement intended to be legally binding.

119

Specimen contract* of the type often used in the Sale/Purchase of a Shop

THIS AGREEMENT made the .... day of .... One thousand nine hundred and .... BETWEEN (name of vendor)
Pharmaceutical Chemist (or Grocer or Newsagent, etc.) of (address of vendor) in the County of ....
(Hereinafter called the Vendor) on the one part AND (name of purchaser)

Pharmaceutical Chemist (or Grocer or Newsagent, etc.) of (address of purchaser)
in the County of ....
(hereinafter called the Purchaser) of the other part WHEREAS the Vendor has for sometime past carried on the business of a Chemist and Druggist (or Grocer or Newsagent, etc.) at
.... in the County of ....
as aforesaid which premises are held by him under a lease dated the ....
.... day of ....One thousand nine hundred and ....
for a period of .... years commencing from the .... day of .... One thousand nine hundred and .... at a rental of £.....
(..........) per annum exclusive of rates subject to the covenants and conditions therein contained
Now it is hereby agreed as follows:–

THE VENDOR will sell and the Purchaser will purchase
Firstly the unexpired interest of the Vendor in the lease hereinbefore mentioned
Secondly the goodwill of the Vendor in connection with the business of a Pharmaceutical Chemist (or Grocer or Newsagent, etc.) now carried on by him at .... in the County of .... as aforesaid together with all trade marks (if any) prescription books and other books (excluding books of account) and papers appertaining to the business and formulae connected therewith also at the option of the Purchaser the benefit of any contracts that may have been entered into by or on behalf of the Vendor
Thirdly all tenants fixtures and fittings loose effects instruments trade utensils chattels and receptacles for drugs in and about the said premises
Fourthly the whole of the good clean and saleable stock-in-trade in and about the premises on the date of completion hereinafter stated

*Adapted from data kindly supplied by Messrs. George, Orridge & Co., Stocktakers, Valuers and Business Transfer Agents, Epping and Associate Offices at Bournemouth, Leeds, Walsall and Glasgow.

THE price for the premises firstly and secondly before described shall be the sum of £...... (......) and for the premises thirdly and fourthly before described the amount of a valuation to be determined by
....
acting as experts and whose decision shall be final and conclusive and legally binding The said valuation shall be carried out at the joint expense of the Vendor and the Purchaser

A deposit of £...... (......) has been paid by the Purchaser to
....
and in part payment of the purchase money as aforesaid

ALL rent rates and other apportionable outgoings of every description shall be apportioned between the parties as on the completion date hereinafter stated

THE purchase shall be completed on the .... day of ....
One thousand nine hundred and ...... herein called the completion date at .... in the County of .... as aforesaid or at such other place as shall be agreed upon by the parties at which time and place the Purchaser shall pay to the Vendor the further sum of ....
and the Vendor will allow the Purchaser to enter into possession of the said premises and will deliver to him all stock-in-trade fixtures fittings instruments chattels utensils and effects hereby agreed to be sold The balance of the purchase money shall be paid by the Purchaser to the Vendor immediately the said .... have declared the amount of the said valuation In the event of the amount already paid by the Purchaser to the Vendor (including the deposit referred to in clause (3) hereof) exceeding the total ascertained purchase price of the business the difference shall forthwith be refunded by the Vendor to the Purchaser

PENDING the completion of the purchase the Vendor shall carry on the said business to the best advantage and all profits and receipts and all outgoings in respect thereof up to the date of completion shall belong to and be paid and discharged by the Vendor and if for any cause the purchase shall not be completed on the completion date the business shall continue to be carried on by the Vendor to the best advantage until the date of actual completion and the Vendor shall be entitled to all profits and receipts and shall discharge all outgoings in respect thereof until such actual completion In such event the outgoings referred to in Clause Four hereof shall be apportioned as at such actual date of completion

7. ALL liabilities in respect of the said business as at the date of completion as aforesaid shall be discharged by the Vendor who shall indemnify the Purchaser in respect thereof and any book debts owing to him as at that date shall for a period of two months following the completion date hereinbefore stated be collected by the Purchaser and paid over to the Vendor at intervals to be agreed upon less a collecting discount of 5% (five per centum) Following the expiration of the said two months the Vendor shall be at liberty to himself collect any debts that may be outstanding provided that before any legal proceedings are taken by the Vendor's Solicitors for the recovery of any debt or debts the Vendor shall confer thereon with the Purchaser who shall be given the option of purchasing the aforesaid debt or debts at a figure to be agreed should he so desire

8. THE Vendor shall forthwith obtain from the Lessor of the property at .... as aforesaid all necessary licences or consents to assign the said lease to the Purchaser and on completion of the transaction as aforesaid shall execute in favour of the Purchaser an assignment of the said lease In the event of such licences or consents not being obtainable this agreement shall be null and void and the said deposit returned to the Purchaser but without any costs or compensation

9. IN addition to any covenant implied by law if the purchase of the said goodwill lease fittings stock and other property referred to herein shall be completed the Vendor hereby undertakes that he will not for a period of ..... years be engaged concerned or interested either alone or jointly or in partnership with or as manager agent servant director or member of any other person firm or company or otherwise in the business of a Pharmaceutical Chemist (or Grocer or Newsagent, etc.) within a radius of ..... miles from .... in the County of .... as aforesaid or permit or suffer his name to be used in any such connection

10. THIS Agreement is subject to the usual routine searches in respect of the said premises which will be made in due course by the Purchaser's Solicitors producing results showing that the premises are clear of any encumbrances or restrictions not shown in the said lease to which reasonable exception might be taken and in the event of any encumbrances or restrictions coming to light the Purchaser shall have the option of withdrawing from the agreement and of reclaiming his deposit but without any costs or compensation

N.B. There are important differences between Scottish and English Law.

Before you enter into a contract of *any* type you should ask yourself and ask your advisors what would happen if you wished to withdraw from the contract. Would it be possible, how would it be possible, what could it cost in cash and in other ways? Always plan in advance for the possibility of matters going awry and have alternatives. This is not pessimism but wisdom.

Short explanatory notes on clauses in the specimen contract:–

CLAUSE 1
Pharmacies have prescription books. Several types of business have books individual to them.

CLAUSE 2
The price is given in figures and words and the name and address of the professional valuers is inserted.

CLAUSE 3
The amount of the desposit, in figures and words, is inserted. Remember the deposit should normally have been made "subject to contract".

CLAUSE 4
Rent, for example, is usually paid quarterly; the purchaser is responsible for his or her share as from the day he or she takes over.

CLAUSE 5
The further sum to be paid at this stage will often have to be based on the total *estimated* purchase price and will take into account the deposit already paid. The total price can frequently only be *estimated* as the result of the valuation of stock, etc., might not be immediately available. In certain cases much further office work is required to be done by the Valuers *after* the stock, etc., has been recorded in the shop.

CLAUSE 6
Your solicitor will explain the significance of "completion date" and "take-over date". These are *not invariably the same.*

CLAUSE 7
If you buy a shop and there are outstanding debts owing by customers to the vendor, you might not want him to take court action against any customer from whom it was difficult to get money owing. It could damage the business

and your goodwill as the new owner if this action were taken. You might, as purchaser, think it in your best interests to buy the debts the vendor had difficulty with, and to deal with the matter yourself. What you agreed to pay for the debts would depend on various circumstances, including what you thought were the chances of collecting them and the time and trouble which might be involved.

CLAUSE 8

The lessor is whoever has let (or leased) the property to the vendor. If the lease cannot be transferred to the would-be purchaser of the shop he will probably decide not to go ahead, but please refer back to Chapter 11.

CLAUSE 9

This contains a "restrictive covenant".

The restriction is designed to protect a buyer against a vendor who might, without such a clause, compete with the purchaser and try to take back all or part of the goodwill he had sold to him (i.e. to the purchaser). A buyer has to be careful that he does not seek *too much* protection.

Buyer and seller must have legal advice about the time and distance for which the parties give and seek protection.

The restriction must be reasonable as between the parties (i.e. the buyer and seller), and also as regards the public. Unless both these conditions are met, the restrictive covenant would normally be completely thrown out, (NOT just amended), by a Court. The purchaser could then be left with no protection whatsoever. What is "reasonable" depends on the particular circumstances of any case.

CLAUSE 10

Your solicitor would explain this. The purpose is to safeguard a purchaser in case something adverse to him and not revealed in the lease, comes to light. Sometimes the lease *itself* contains restrictions a buyer cannot accept, for instance restrictions on the activities allowed on the premises.

Survey

It is important that when you take a lease you familiarise yourself with the terms so that you know precisely what your obligations are as regards rent, rates, repairs, decorations, insurances, etc.

A survey is advisable and this will tell you what work if any is needed and when. A schedule of condition should be prepared so that there is a formal record of the state of the premises when you took over. Otherwise you might find you are asked to make good defects already existing when you became the tenant and that you eventually restore the premises to the landlord in better condition than when you entered them. As a general rule a tenant is obliged at the end of a lease to return premises in substantially the same condition, but allowing for fair wear and tear, as when he or she took them over. You must protect yourself against going to the expense of putting right something for which you could rightly avoid responsibility.

Your solicitor's guidance and a survey are crucial: this applies also when you are considering purchase of a freehold.

Chapter 29
RETURN ON CAPITAL:
CHOICE: ALTERNATIVES: D.C.F.

Economic problems exist because our resources are scarce in relation to our demands; we cannot have everything we want, so we have to choose between various alternatives. Some resources can be used only in one or a few ways, but others can be applied to many different ends; we might have difficulty in deciding which objectives are to have priority.

As we have this situation of needing to choose, something is sacrificed in order that something else can be gained. Hence, in economic terms, the *real* cost of anything is what we have given up to obtain it. The cost, say, of a car is not (in real terms) the money we pay for it, but the furniture or holiday or swimming-pool we could alternatively have bought.

When you consider purchase of a shop you have many choices to make. First of all you must ask whether a shop is the "best" investment for you, taking into account both financial and non-financial factors. You will be wise to work out the return on your capital from a shop, comparing this with returns elsewhere than in retail. Then you will compare returns on capital in various shops. Finally you will compare returns from alternative investments within a business, in stock, in fixtures, in training, in advertising, and so on.

Some decisions are substantially "all or nothing", while others are what the economists call "marginal". Either you buy a specific new car or you do not, but you can and indeed will normally need to have both stock *and* fixtures, the question being how much to spend on each.

The more efficient you are as a business person, the less you will feel afterwards that you should have spent more on one thing and less on another. We try to reach a balance where the last few pounds or last few hundred pounds invested in each of two or more directions, give us equal "marginal" satisfaction.

If you already own a business, your capital investment is what you can sell the business for as a going concern in the current market *now*, NOT necessarily what you paid for it. And if you are buying a shop, your capital investment is what you pay for it *now;* what your investment is at any future time will depend on the market *then*. So the market decides.

When considering any capital investment it can help to apply the D.C.F. or Discounted Cash Flow principle. The basic and simple concept behind this principle is that money *now* is usually worth more than money in the future, that if you are given, say, £1,000 today, it could grow to (say) £1,050 in one year and, at compound interest of 5 per cent per annum, double itself in between 14-15 years. The *present* value of £1.00 in 14-15 years is therefore, on the basis of 5 per cent compound interest paid annually, about 50p. With higher interest rates, the present value is of course less, and conversely.

Other factors than interest rates should be considered when assessing an investment; these factors include profitability of various forms of investment, taxation, forecast changes in the purchasing power of money, depreciation rates, cost of supervising the investment, the residual value of any investment, and so forth. It is important to study the prospects for deflation or inflation, expected trends of prices generally and of prices of shops in particular, to examine markets broadly and in the specific sphere of the business under analysis.

A study of D.C.F. can stimulate a realistic attitude to investment in a shop, in fixtures and fittings, in stock, in training, and so on. It can help an investor to understand just what return he might obtain for taking risk.

A valuable discipline to carry out is to calculate the expected return over a number of years from each of several alternative investments. Bring the forecast profit for each year back to *present day* value by discounting it on a compound interest, acceptable return on capital, basis. Each year must be calculated separately and discounted for the relevant number of years.

Helpful comparisons can now be made when the *total* discounted forecast profits over a period, for each type of investment, are known. Take into account the *residual* value (if any) at the end of the period in each case, discounting this value back to current value. It is essential to take into your reckoning the *expenses* relating to each alternative investment, not forgetting the cost of *time*.

The period for which you calculate might be, for example, the length of your lease, the time to your retirement, the time until you intend to sell the business, the expected useful life of fixtures, etc. You will obviously use the same period of time for each alternative you are comparing *or* calculate the return on investment as so much percentage per year.

As to taxation, an essential point is to be *consistent* when making comparisons between differing investments, i.e. making calculations *after* tax in every case, or *before* tax in every case.

Be consistent similarly about expected changes in money value due to inflation or deflation.

As much of the D.C.F. calculation must be based on *expectation and forecast,* we must not treat it as *exact,* but as an indicator on broad lines. Do not expect the technique to provide marginally close decisions on investment policy: it *can* assist you to avoid grossly unrealistic use of resources. Naturally, the further ahead you are forecasting, the greater the risk of inaccuracy.

Care is needed on the point of residual value. A lease, or a set of fixtures, is usually a depreciating asset, but goodwill might appreciate with time. *Whenever* you buy a shop, you should look ahead to when you might want to sell and should try to make as reasoned as possible a forecast of values and markets *then*.

A Pioneer Service for Retailers

If you are in business you have problems of staffing, training, stock investment, marketing, competition, and so on. Your problems are *unique*. General principles can help you find solutions, but how often do they *fully* apply to your business?

The service I offer is personal and individual.

Most business problems arise, I believe, through human frailty – from *lack of* knowledge, enthusiasm, co-operation, will and communication, from lack of confidence. So in tackling problems we must think first of the *people* involved. We must also understand difficulties due to shortage of time and money.

Why do staff leave, why do incentives fail, why do sales hopes and expected profit margins fade? What can you do about these disappointments?

Perhaps you should consider your own attitudes and outlook, review your business techniques and use of time and other resources, human and material? You are maybe already efficient and go-ahead; such retailers are often the ones to be most ardent for *further* success.

Do you find that to talk about a problem, to define it clearly, is in itself helpful? If you have a business worry or idea you would like to discuss, please give me a ring as suggested ahead.

Here are a few typical cases where consultation could be valuable:

IF –you are thinking of opening a new shop or of closing an existing one.

your sales are failing to keep pace with overheads, or your gross margin is fluctuating or declining.

you have too much money invested in stock.

your wages and salaries are uneconomically high.

you have several businesses and find co-ordination difficult.

you find it hard to get the full co-operation of staff and colleagues in promoting your ideas.

Consultation is available for specific short-term problems or on a longer term basis. Sometimes a single interview suffices; in other cases much research is needed.

If you have a business idea or worry to discuss, if a problem is *developing*, please– 'PHONE ME – if we *both* believe I could help I will tell you how I work.

Make an APPOINTMENT – I am flexible about time and place.

You can rely on my frankness as to whether I feel I can be of use to you. If your problem is not for me, possibly I can suggest someone else to try.

Success with your problems I cannot of course *guarantee*. I can promise to listen with sympathy and to give an honest opinion.

E. A. Jensen.

Chapter 30
A FINAL SUMMING UP

We now list a few salient thoughts on the investigation of a business. The following are worthy of special emphasis.

1. The need for knowledge of:

(a) yourself and your requirements;

(b) the business itself and the market as a whole;

(c) local and general conditions.

2. Every shop is unique in some qualities.

3. The valuing of a business calls for judgment and imagination as well as knowledge.

4. Figures alone can mislead; seek out the background, the facts they represent.

5. *The market at the time* governs the price of businesses, as of anything.

6. Rules have their exceptions, but you will deal more effectively with the unusual if you are competent with the usual.

7. We have suggested a method and approach suitable to the problem; there is no easy "rule of thumb" way.

8. Only by applying ideas *in practice* to definite problems, will you become quicker and more certain; this book does not offer an armchair method.

9. Indecision can normally be overcome through adequate knowledge.

10. The man who is not prepared to take a risk cannot expect to make a profit. You should, however, try to reduce as far as you can the risk in relation to the possible reward.

11. *You alone can decide* what amount of risk you are able and willing to take, bearing in mind your particular financial and other circumstances and your own temperament and character.

12. It is essential to keep up-to-date on changing legislation, etc.

13. Make your professional advisers collaborators in your business and keep in close touch with them.

14. Run your shop with clearly-defined objectives; plan ahead; do not wait for crises before you act, but try to foresee and avoid them.

YOUR BUSINESS ANALYSIS NOTES ⟶

Name and Address (or Ref. No.)	Turnover (3 years figures each business where possible)	Gross profit as % of turnover	Adjusted net profit as % of turnover	Pure profit as % of turnover	Total price of business	Pure profit as % of total price	at cost divided by average stock	Fixed overheads as % of turnover	Variable overheads as % of turnover	lease/goodwill divided by pure profit
Year ended										
Year ended										
Year ended										
Year ended										
Year ended										
Year ended										
Year ended										
Year ended										
Year ended										
Averages for Businesses 1-3										

Remarks

133

Name and Address (or Ref. No.)	Turnover (3 years figures each business where possible)	Gross profit as % of turnover	Adjusted net profit as % of turnover	Pure profit as % of turnover	Total price of business	Pure profit as % of total price	Turnover at cost divided by average stock	Fixed overheads as % of turnover	Variable overheads as % of turnover	Price of lease/goodwill divided by pure profit
	Year ended									
	Year ended									
	Year ended									
	Year ended									
	Year ended									
	Year ended									
	Year ended									
	Year ended									
	Year ended									
Averages for Businesses 1-6										

Remarks

Name and Address (or Ref. No.)		Turnover (3 years figures each business where possible)	Gross profit as % of turnover	Adjusted net profit as % of turnover	Pure profit as % of turnover	Total price of business	Pure profit as % of total price	at cost divided by average stock	Fixed overheads as % of turnover	Variable overheads as % of turnover	Price of lease/goodwill divided by pure profit
	Year ended										
	Year ended										
	Year ended										
	Year ended										
	Year ended										
	Year ended										
	Year ended										
	Year ended										
	Year ended										
Averages for Businesses 1 - 9											

Remarks

Name and Address (or Ref. No.)		Turnover (3 years figures each business where possible)	Gross profit as % of turnover	Adjusted net profit as % of turnover	Pure profit as % of turnover	Total price of business	Pure profit as % of total price	Turnover at cost divided by average stock	Fixed overheads as % of turnover	Variable overheads as % of turnover	Price of lease/goodwill divided by pure profit
	Year ended										
	Year ended										
	Year ended										
	Year ended										
	Year ended										
	Year ended										
	Year ended										
	Year ended										
	Year ended										
Averages for Businesses 1-12											

Remarks

APPENDIX

Appendix

AN EXERCISE IN FORECASTING

When you buy a shop or any other business you are backing your judgment that the concern will provide the profits and other benefits you expect. So you are in effect trying to see into the future and to reduce uncertainties.

While profit is the reward for risk successfully undertaken, and while risk is part of life, many shop buyers fail to keep the uncertainty down as much as they could. The main reasons for this failure are lack of sufficient facts and lack of careful interpretation of the facts.

Forecasting is a key part of market research, and one of the most valuable assets a businessman or woman can possess or acquire is the ability to form a shrewd judgment on the likely future of an existing shop or one to be started. Prophecy cannot ensure success but it can often help you avoid disaster.

In this chapter we aim to make forecasting a practical exercise for the prospective owner of a shop, to suggest how information can be gathered under various headings and how it can be applied to your individual situation. Once certain general principles and procedures have been outlined it is for you to decide what is of value to you in your unique position.

We should be careful to distinguish fact from opinion and to be as objective as we can; we should be prepared to change our mind about what we want if our research indicates this would be sensible. The kind of forecasting proposed calls for collection and interpretation of data: the result might be to confirm you in the type of shop you have in mind or to turn your search into new directions. You must of course strike a balance between being so confused by a mass of facts and advice that you find it hard to come to a decision, and taking too hasty a decision because you are not willing to investigate before you invest. Information should be used to clarify, not to confuse.

It is worth reminding ourselves at this stage that the perfect shop does not exist, that we will not obtain everything we want. But the kind of investigation already suggested in this book, plus the forecasting exercise now described, should help you get much closer to your desires.

Whether you are young or old, whether you expect to run the shop you purchase for only a few or for many years, the long term future can still be of great importance. Even if you think you will want to sell in a few years it will pay you to buy something which will offer potential to your successor and thus make the shop more readily saleable and valuable. Whenever we buy we should have selling in the back of our mind.

For wise forecasting you need:
(1) Information and opinion.
(2) Judgment to decide what information and opinion is relevant to *you*.
(3) The ability to draw logical conclusions from the data.
(4) The wisdom to draw correct conclusions from the evidence.
(5) A healthy doubt about anything that is presented to you as a certainty, and the judgment to weigh the odds.
(6) The readiness to listen to advice if you cannot make up your mind over a problem, together with the realisation that not every problem has a solution to suit everyone.

The many factors, indicators, and trends we shall look at can basically be considered from the viewpoints of time and space. We need, for instance, to ask ourselves *when* and at what rate influences on the future of the shop will occur, and from what area the influences will come. Suppose you believe that new technology will radically alter the prospects for the type of goods and services you will be handling, you must assess when, how quickly, the technology will come, and whether the effects will be favourable, unfavourable, or about neutral. Or if you are set on buying a village petrol station with shop, how far are you to be influenced by the debate about the future of oil supplies, of world trends in energy? Will you consider events thousands of miles away or only the pattern of car ownership etc. in the immediate locality of the village? However large or small the venture you are planning you should at least be alive to the far away influences, far away in time and space, as well as to the factors on the doorstep. You can usefully call on the work-study questions of WHEN, WHERE, HOW, WHAT, WHO, and WHY when examining factors and trends; they can be thought-provoking and an aid to clear focusing on problems.

In most if not all retail businesses there is provided a mixture of services and goods; shops vary from those where service is small to those where the cost of the merchandise is tiny in relation to the advisory element. Compare an electrical/electronics repair-service retailer with say a news/tobacconist shopkeeper sited where speed of service is the key factor.

In addition to considering time and space in relation to the forecasting factors it is worth keeping in mind the advantages and disadvantages of the mainly service and the mainly merchandise shops referred to in the previous paragraph. In the "service" shop the gross margin could be very high, but there could be heavy investment in equipment and in the training needed before one can conduct such a shop. The stock might be low and display might not be so important as in the "goods" shop. The latter might or might not call for the expert knowledge the "service" outlet can require but stock-holding could be large and equipment investment substantial, although of a different type from that in the "service" concern.

In every type of shop close attention must be given to the degree of likelihood that changes in technology will be dominant in deciding events.

Forecasting is a complex job because retailing is so integral a part of life in our society; few, if any, things happen politically, socially, legally, etc. without there being some impact on the shopkeeper. What I suggest is that you check through the lists which follow and pick out those pointers most likely to influence your judgment as to what shop you want to buy. Also consider factors and trends likely to affect the future of supporting shops in the vicinity and of local industries, etc. Although the factors have been classified under several headings it will be appreciated that many of them could come under more than one classification.

Here are the main groups with factors in each of them, some factors occurring in more than one group. The groups are followed by a list of *trends* or influences; the *movement* of events so far can sometimes help us foresee future probabilities or possibilities.

ECONOMIC
Factors

population, size and composition
employment
industrial output
inflation/deflation, money supply
unemployment, and regional variations
terms of trade and imports/exports
wholesale prices
capitalisation and profitability of industry
value of the pound
average earnings
consumer spending
productivity, gross national and gross domestic product
E.E.C. influences on economic matters
rents and rates, levels, and official policies
taxation
interest rates
income distribution
banking figures, loans, etc.
stock levels
state expenditure
house prices and number being built
mortgages and mortgage rates
expendable income
tourism
immigration, emigration
company results and share movements
investment in industry
building society figures
life assurance, new business, etc.
consumer loans by finance houses and by retailers
hire purchase figures
personal assets
personal savings
personal income and expenditure

MARKETING
Factors
world trade and markets
transport and communication
advertising
new towns, hypermarkets, etc.
mail order selling
selling in the home (selling "parties", etc.)
shopping by computer

SOCIAL
Factors
education (technical and other)
social services
workers/dependants ratios
E.E.C. influences on social habits, etc.
leisure pursuits
life expectancy
birth/death rates
size of families and types of family
poverty and destitution
shop and other opening hours
population movements, large cities, development areas
unions and unionisation, participation, profit sharing
holiday travel
commuting
dishonesty and security measures
working from home
class barriers
alcohol consumption
tobacco consumption
health and diet, slimming
sports and hobbies
animals, pets
small business
self-employment
increasing power of minorities
eating habits

proportion of old-age pensioners
cremation and burial
living standards
sex equality
"unisex"
permissiveness
pornography

POLITICAL
Factors
government attitudes and policies
common market and E.E.C. attitudes and policies
tax raising levies such as the prescription levy
political ideologies
budget policies and taxation
degree of dependence on state departments as customer

LEGAL
Factors
legislation affecting retailers in general and particular sections
legal points peculiar to an individual shop, e.g. covenants in a lease, clauses
  in a sale/purchase contract, etc.
clauses in any partnership or other contract
legal restrictions on trading, e.g. need to have a qualification or to
  be registered
shop opening hours laid down by law, and restrictions on goods to be sold at
  particular times
liability for products sold, or for services
legal or quasi-legal controls on advertising, e.g. as for cigarettes
resale price maintenance
codes of ethics which might ultimately have legal backing
licensing or registration of traders
consumer protection through Sale of Goods Act and other legislation

PERSONAL, PSYCHOLOGICAL, PHYSICAL
Factors
health, age, etc.
qualifications
personality

experience and training

capital and other resources

relationship with others involved in your purchase and conduct of a shop

job satisfaction sought

personal priorities regarding money, leisure, etc.

TECHNOLOGICAL AND GENERAL

Factors

current ideology, attitude of the public to shops, to business in general, to the particular type of shop under consideration

impact of the "chip", of computers, of new sources of information and of access to them through television, etc.

pattern of retail distribution: ordering by computer

stock control and ordering systems and effects of new technology

developments in communication, audio and visual

energy situation and implications

possibilities related to space exploration

natural factors such as danger of flooding, subsidence, etc., and in certain areas, proximity to hazardous processes

industry patterns, changes in occupations and their location

fashion

activities of leading retailers in various fields

car registrations

wage or salary earners and number of dependants

prospective growth in social services

weather and climate

cinemas and theatres, etc., numbers and attendances

TRENDS

Here are some trends which seem likely to affect the pattern of retailing: it is suggested that you add to this list any trends you have yourself noticed, trends which apply to retailing in general and also those particularly important to the type of shop you are considering and to the supporting shops:—

the trend towards do-it-yourself activities which has been growing for many years and which extends in new directions.

the trend towards energy saving, the increasing use of cycles for transport, etc.

the trend towards smaller families.

the trend towards home ownership.

the trend towards working from home and the likely encouragement of this by developments in communication, computerisation, audio-visual facilities, the "chip", etc., cost of transport, etc.

the trend to increased consumption of wines.

the trend towards leisure activities and foreign travel.

the trend towards demanding personal attention and service, individual treatment.

trends in crime, in amount and in kind.

trends towards a fall in the amount of food grown by allotment holders.

trends in the number employed in the public sector.

trends to sex equality (and related attitudes).

trends towards large shops, hypermarkets, etc., "one stop" shopping, with another trend to small specialist shops.

the trend towards self-employment and small business.

This list is intended as an indication only of the kinds of movements in behaviour and attitude which affect, to greater or less degree, what happens in retailing. We are all shopkeepers or shoppers, and hundreds of thousands of us are both. It can be very revealing for a shopkeeper to study his or her own behaviour as a shopper.

After you have considered the lists of factors and trends put before you and after you have added your own information and views, you could, I believe, find it useful to spend a little time on the exercise now briefly described; the cooperation of anyone else involved with you in your plans would be valuable.

EXERCISE

(1) Check through the lists of factors and trends, to which you have added your own. Select those factors and trends most related to what you have in mind.

(2) Decide as closely as you can on the *relative* importance of the factors and trends chosen. The ratings could be say from one to ten, with one for the least important and ten for the most. If there is one overriding factor then clearly your choice of a shop will be governed by that even if there are many reasons against the choice. For example, if you have decided that your shop must be in some particular small village or resort you will have to accept any disadvantages this brings with it.

145

(3) Decide, as accurately as you can, how likely any trend or factor you have chosen is to continue, and whether the factor or trend is favourable, neutral, or unfavourable to the shop you seek or are already investigating. Rate the likelihood one to ten.

(4) Make out a table with each factor and trend, rated one to ten in importance and also rated one to ten according to how certain or uncertain you think it is. Have one column for favourable, one for unfavourable, one for neutral, factors and trends. You might feel the neutral items do not need to be included.

(5) You can now draw up a "balance sheet" something on the following lines, each rating for importance being multiplied by the rating for likelihood, with totals of favourable and unfavourable influences.

Specimen "Balance Sheet" Table   [*theoretical for illustration only*]

Factor or Trend	Impor- tance (a)	Proba- bility (b)	score (a × b)	Analysed forecast effects		
				good*	neutral	bad*
rise in living standards	8	6	good 48	48		
increase in holiday travel	7	8	good 56	56		
rise in "Do it yourself"	10	8	good 80	80		
*increase in car registrations	9	6	good 54	54		
*energy saving [swing to cycling]	7	8	bad 56			56
total scores				238		56

* "good" or "bad" *from the viewpoint of the shop concerned* and its merchandise. If you sell cycles then increase in cars might be "bad" and swing to

cycles "good". Similarly in other cases "good" or "bad" is a matter of viewpoint.

Notes

The table should be as simple as possible, by *not* including more than a small number of factors and trends in the first case. If necessary, more could be included in a further table if no clear pattern comes from the first exercise.

The table is intended as an *aid* to making decisions: it cannot provide a decision, as judgment must be applied to the findings, which are a guide only. Judgment and knowledge will naturally have been used in fixing ratings and in choosing factors and trends.

It would be imprudent to try and reach a decision solely because the "balance sheet" proves either favourable or unfavourable. I suggest that carrying out the exercise helps to highlight points which can be overlooked or under- or over-emphasised if a written summary is not made. The attempt alone to deal with the matters raised by studying this exercise can be most fruitful. Each factor and trend should be considered from the TIME and SPACE viewpoints already referred to.

New or modified factors and trends can be expected, so it is imperative that you keep up-to-date your knowledge of these by studying trade papers and every source of information and opinion you can find time to peruse. Business and other affairs change rapidly and success depends more and more on adaptability and the willingness to give a fair hearing to new ideas.

If you can find out what people want, or can be persuaded to want, something you can provide at an acceptable profit and under conditions you are ready to accept, you have a crucial key to successful shopkeeping. And the more you can look ahead the more assured can be your future.

You might find it necessary to train yourself in new skills if those you already have do not appear likely to give you the returns you seek, if the trends are making them of less and less value. You should ask how you can best compete by supplying what competitors do not offer, by close study of what is happening in the branch of retailing which interests you.

The time to carry out the research suggested is *before* you buy. Remember to relate all your plans to your own material and non-material needs and

147

priorities, not forgetting those people involved with you. Make a careful distinction between needs and wants, as regards yourself and the public.

Beware of averages which are used carelessly. You can learn much from broad general information, but you must get down to the specific case of the shop you have in mind and your own circumstances.

In addition to the considerations of TIME and SPACE emphasised in this chapter, decide what is within and what is outside your control, what you can change and what you cannot hope to alter in the various factors and trends.

There is, I believe, a prosperous and fulfilling future in retailing for those ready to meet the challenges and to do the research which is the groundwork for wise selection of a shop. If you decide to offer some unusual type of service and/or merchandise, for example, to operate a shop open during the evening until midnight or beyond and with a variety of merchandise of the emergency kind, this could fill a need and be profitable; there could however be problems over re-selling, as many buyers of shops might not accept what some regard as "unsocial working hours". As against this, some buyers might be particularly attracted to the unusual. The market, supply and demand, must be respected, and whenever you buy think ahead to when you might want to sell.

To conclude on a note of optimism and encouragement:—let me remind you that to invest in a shop can be one of the least costly ways of becoming your own employer, and one of the most satisfying of occupations for anyone who basically likes people. And in addition to profits and satisfaction and a worthwhile job you can, if you act wisely, build up a capital gain as a bonus for your efforts. You will normally get out in proportion to what you have put in:—choose a shop sensibly and then run it efficiently.

SUPPLEMENT
The Balance Sheet

Many business people, even some with long experience of running a shop, do not realise how much crucial information can be gained by thorough study of balance sheets. Nor do they know the limitations of a balance sheet, what it does *not* show.

Earlier in this book it was stated that while the profit and loss account details what has happened in a shop over a period of time, the balance sheet indicates what the shop owns and what it owes at a specified date. Thus the profit and loss account might be for the year (or six months or other period) ended say March 31st. The corresponding balance sheet would show assets and liabilities, (i.e. what the business owns and owes) at March 31st. The profit and loss account is part of the accounts, while the balance sheet is not. The balance sheet does however use information extracted from the accounting system.

It is important to understand that the balance sheet includes only assets and liabilities which can be valued in money terms. In many businesses the people working in them are the most valuable assets, while in some there might be staff who are more of a liability than an asset. The balance sheet will not help here. Similarly, the reputation of a shop could be of great or of trivial value, worthless or worth less than nothing: the balance sheet will not indicate which.

When a prospective buyer is trying to place a value on the goodwill of a shop he or she cannot do so solely by investigating the accounts and balance sheet. Concrete assets such as stock and fixtures and intangibles like goodwill and potential must be taken into reckoning if a wise assessment and choice of shop is to be made.

The arrangement of balance sheets varies but this need not cause difficulty so long as the investigator knows what to look for.

Any balance sheet you examine should give: –
the name of the business—the date of the balance sheet—the basis of the valuations (e.g: "stock as valued by XYZ valuers")—the auditor's certificate.

A balance sheet should be clear and comply with legal requirements.

Every asset, every liability, must it is stressed, be closely scrutinised. Investigate for instance the true present value of goodwill along the lines put forward in this book. In some balance sheets goodwill is not shown as an asset or has been depreciated, while in others it might appear at a figure well above the current market value. What about the debtors? Are they reliable or are there doubtful payers among them? How old are the debts? Check on the value shown and on who fixed the value, for each asset.

With the liabilities, make sure you find out when they are due for payment, the terms for repayment of any loan, the interest rate etc. Be especially vigilant as to whether there is any undisclosed or contingent liability. Is there a legal action pending or expected against the business, is there in existence some possibly unprofitable contract for supply or purchase of goods? Is the shop committed to buy from a particular supplier who has perhaps helped to finance the vendor? The importance of some of these points will vary according to whether you are buying shares of a limited company or the assets only of either a limited company or of a non-limited liability business.

If you buy the shares of a company you inherit the liabilities as well as the assets. On the other hand, when you simply buy the assets, whether of a limited company or of a non-limited concern, such as lease/goodwill, fixtures/fittings etc. and stock, you do not take responsibility for any debts, contracts, or other commitments of the vendor unless this is specifically arranged. Arguments for and against taking over shares in a limited company or forming a company can be complex and the matter is very much one for individual decision according to your unique circumstances. Discuss fully with your accountant.

The balance sheet shows only, I emphasise, those items of which the value can be assessed in money. But money itself is not constant in value in real terms year by year or even sometimes day by day. The discounted-cash-flow principle has been outlined elsewhere in this book and should be kept in mind when studying cash values. Never regard money as you would a pound weight or a kilo, a foot or a metre, all permanent and definite. A further complication is that changes in the value of money do not affect all items to the same extent.

There is sometimes difficulty in understanding why the capital a purchaser invests in a shop appears as a liability, not as an asset, on the balance sheet. The point to bear in mind is that a business, whether a limited company or not, should be looked upon as having its own existence, as being a kind of "person" quite distinct from the owner. When you buy the assets of a shop or start a new shop you, as a person, are lending to the business as a separate "person" the money you put in. So the business owes the money to you and it is shown as a liability of the business. The cash is *your asset* but the *shop's liability*.

The assets and liabilities in a balance sheet are normally listed in a special way. Assets are by convention arranged so that at one end of the list is the asset most readily convertible into cash and at the other end the asset most difficult so to convert. The other assets are listed in between in order of "liquidity". The more readily an asset can be turned into cash the more liquid it is. Money itself is perfectly liquid and thus appears at one end in the specimen balance sheet. Money in the bank is almost as liquid as cash in the till, but money owing by customers and money tied up in stock is less liquid and that invested in a car or van less liquid still. Goodwill is generally not convertible into cash until the shop or part of it is sold, while fixtures/ fittings etc. usually rank somewhere between goodwill and stock for liquidity.

The liabilities are by custom listed with those which have to be paid first at one end of the list and those to be paid last at the other. If the business terminates or is sold the owner or shareholders come last for settlement of their dues: sometimes they receive nothing if there are not enough assets to clear other liabilities. In a successful business, however, the capital originally invested could multiply many times because the assets have built up to give a large excess over liabilities apart from the owner's capital.

We have shown merely one of the ways in which a balance sheet might be set out. Sometimes assets and liabilities are shown one above the other, not side by side, and often they are sub-divided into different types. The most common division is into so-called "fixed" and so-called "current" assets and liabilities. Current assets and liabilities are normally those which can be turned into cash or have to be paid within a year. Goodwill and property and fixtures/fittings etc. are examples of fixed assets, while stock and cash are current assets. The capital of the owner is a fixed liability as is a long-term mortgage, but money owed to trade suppliers and for such items as rent and rates is a current liability.

It is important to compare current assets with current liabilities. This reveals the liquidity of a shop, that is it shows how promptly short-term debts can be met. As a rule current assets should be sufficient to cover current liabilities: otherwise a business can be in serious financial difficulty even though it has plenty of total assets to cover total liabilities. A business is solvent if total assets equal or exceed total liabilities but creditors are not always prepared to wait for their money and often cannot afford to as this would give them their own liquidity problems. One person's asset is someone else's liability.

Clearly we should always examine closely how assets are made up as well as their total. Similarly find out what liabilities call for early payment and which are long-term.

Current assets can be further split between "quick" current assets and the rest. Examples of "quick" current assets are cash in hand and at the bank, and safe customer accounts. Stock, while a current asset, is not usually regarded as a "quick" asset.

Fixed assets are generally depreciated as most assets fall in value with the passage of time or with use: by contrast certain ones such as antiques and property and others can increase in value. A buyer should find out whether each asset is shown at cost or at current market cost, who valued it, and the basis for any depreciation. Depreciation could be based on time, so much per year, on use, so much per mile, or in other ways appropriate to the item. The point is to ascertain *how*. Special attention should be given to goodwill, which might be worth a vastly different sum from anything shown on the balance sheet.

When balance sheets are being studied comparisons between different years can be more significant than figures at a single date. For instance, a lower stock level might be matched by a reduced bank overdraft: this could be a healthy sign if the shop had appeared to be overstocked the year before but a bad sign if it meant that trade had fallen off. Figures should not be taken at face value and they should be related to one another and to those for other dates.

Reference has been made to solvency and to liquidity: we can now look at profitability, where the balance sheet is also of great value. Profitability indicates the relationship between profit made and the resources engaged in earning that profit. The balance sheet deals only with what we can value in money and does not state the investment in time, energy, devotion, worry, owners make in their shop. These intangible investments might or might not produce profit in proportion to their amount.

Approaches vary as to how the investment in a business is defined. I suggest that a simple and logical way to tackle this matter and to compare return on investment in different shops is to start by assessing the *current* market value of a shop under investigation *along the lines described in this book*. This market value for lease/goodwill, stock, fixtures/fittings etc.

represents what the owner would have available for investment elsewhere and/or to deal with any debts, if he or she did not have cash tied up in the business. The profit as a percentage of the current market value of the shop is the return on the investment, and this should be compared with the results of similar calculations for as many businesses as possible in the trade. Where freehold properties are involved (as distinct from leases) they should not be included in the market value for our present purpose but should be considered separately. A realistic current rent for any freehold should of course have been charged against the profit. The profit figure to be used in these calculations is the pure profit before tax as employed in method B in chapter twelve, the "yield" method.

The valuation of shares can be a complex matter and professional help is usually needed. Briefly, the value of the ordinary shares is equal to the difference between the value of all the assets, including the current value of lease/goodwill, and of all the liabilities apart from the ordinary shares. To take a simple example let us imagine a limited company where 5000 ordinary £1.00 shares have been issued and no other shares, that the total assets are currently valued at £50,000 and that liabilities apart from the shares total £30,000. In this case the ordinary shares would be worth £4.00 each, that is £50,000 minus £30,000 divided by 5000. In practice things are seldom so simple. There might for instance be several different kinds of share in existence and there could be a variety of conditions which cannot be measured in money but which might still have a strong influence on the value of the shares. And what if liabilities excluding the shares exceed assets?

Figures alone, essential as they are, cannot guide us to a true assessment of shares or of a business. Judgment and imagination are also necessary, the judgment to weigh up risk against prospects of reward and the imagination to detect potential and opportunity. Are there assets which are under valued, assets which could be more profitably employed in other ways? And so forth. The balance sheet does not by itself enable us to forecast accurately the likely level of future profits. To attempt this we should analyse a host of factors as proposed in the appendix "An exercise in forecasting".

Anyone considering purchase of a shop would I suggest be wise to learn, if he or she does not already know, at least the elements of bookkeeping and accounts. Know what information to seek and how to interpret it. And once a shop has been bought an understanding of these matters is essential if the business is to be run and controlled efficiently and if the fullest use is to be made of the specialist services of an accountant. You must know what your accountant is talking about.

Accounts are a powerful aid to business, a means of employing information about the past and present in order to have a more profitable future.

N.B.You might not invariably be given access to the balance sheet (or sheets) of a business you are examining, as they are not part of the accounts. But make sure you are prepared in advance to benefit from any opportunity you are given to inspect them.

Here is a typical balance sheet layout with just a few specimen entries:—

ABC Retail
Balance sheet as at June 30th, 198—

Liabilities	*Assets*
capital account	goodwill
mortgage loan	freehold property
trade accounts (owing by ABC Retail)	fixtures, fittings, etc.
other accounts payable (e.g. telephone, electricity, etc.)	car and van
bank overdraft	stock
taxes	debtors (customers' accounts owing to ABC Retail)
	building society account
	cash in bank
	cash in hand

The illustration is not intended to be complete but only to show how a balance sheet is often presented.

INDEX

INDEX

INDEX *(continued)*

APPENDIX:

  An Exercise in Forecasting, pp. 137–148

SUPPLEMENT:

  The Balance Sheet pp. 149–155

Stock Control

(extracted and adapted from "More Profit from your Stock,"
by E. A. Jensen)

INTRODUCTION

Stock represents **Money**; it must be made to work hard in producing profit; it must constantly be looked at with the question in mind "What return as profit is this stock showing?".

Stock control in its widest sense, over the years as well as over the days, can help to keep a shopkeeper "fluid", that is, with ready money quickly to hand. Stock control enables the retailer to make sure he or she is not holding too much of a limited number of products and failing to offer other saleable goods. Stock problems are customer-service problems, and the retailer can succeed only by close and interested study of those who buy from him and those who could be persuaded to do so.

Service to the public and the skilful use of resources are the smaller retailer's chief weapons in the fight against wealthier rivals.

Stock can give profit only when sold and paid for; if stock is bought at the wrong time or in the wrong way, loss can take the place of profit. To handle stock skilfully we must study our market with the utmost care, as lack of market knowledge is the root of many stock difficulties.

A common fault of retailers is failure to relate closely what is bought with what is sold or hoped to be sold. There is the temptation to look at the profit margin per sale rather than the total profit over time, to consider goods too much from their intrinsic qualities rather than from their saleability in the business concerned.

It is a human failing to over-buy because an extra discount is offered, to carry six months' supply where three weeks' holding would be adequate. There is a right time to buy large quantities with courage and confidence, but stocks are usually too high rather than too low.

What to buy, how much to buy; these are day-to-day worries of the retailer.

Solutions to the problems briefly referred to in this introduction are not simple; they vary from shop to shop and from town to town, as every business is unique.

Certain principles can nevertheless be worked out, and it is then up to each shopkeeper to apply them to his own affairs. No one can help you as you can help yourself, no one can know your business as you do.

Sound principles, adapted to your own shop, will give you firmly-based confidence to compete and will help you to gain the highest profit your resources can produce.

I have emphasised the capital problem of the smaller retailer, but every shopkeeper, small or large, neglects stock control at his or her peril.

Chapter 1

STOCK and SALES. Rate of stock turn. Variety and Sales. Capital and Stock.

One of the hardest questions for any shopkeeper is whether to buy in large quantities to obtain discounts and bonuses, or whether to buy in smaller amounts and turn the stock over more often. There can be no answer which is true for every shop.

Every gain has some accompanying loss, in money or otherwise; you have to decide which policy is, *on balance*, the one to suit your own particular needs, resources, and ambitions.

The first point to consider is what policy you adopt and adapt as to the amount of stock held in relation to your sales. The value of stock will usually vary from day to day, from month to month, and over the years, but in most businesses there is a fairly constant average stock held, at any rate over short periods.

The correct, but not the universal way of relating stock values to sales, is to find out the *cost* of the goods sold in a year, and to divide this by the average value of stock carried during the year, the value again being at *cost* price. We use the period of a year because this is the normal interval employed by shopkeepers for their accounts. The important point is that we must compare the cost of goods sold with stock at cost value. **Always relate Stock to Sales**.

If a retailer's sales for a year are £200,000 at retail prices, that is at the prices to his customers, we must first of all work out what these goods have cost. Suppose that the cost of the goods was £150,000 and that the *average* stock held over the year was, at cost price, £30,000. With these figures the rate of stock turn, as it is called, is £150,000 divided by £30,000 which is 5 (*not* £200,000 divided by £30,000, which is $6\frac{2}{3}$rds).

Sometimes sales at retail prices are compared with stock at retail prices also; this gives the same ratio between our sales and our stock in any particular case, as is obtained by comparing sales at cost with stock at cost. The important thing in calculating the number of stock turns per annum, is to be sure that you are comparing like with like, that is to take sales and stock *both* at cost price or *both* at retail price.

Many retailers have their stock valued at the end of each trading year, and the average stock held is worked out by adding the stock at the beginning of a year to the stock at the end of the year and dividing by two. This method is reasonably satisfactory where stock value does not fluctuate widely during the year, but it is obvious that if a varying stock were valued several times a year we would have a more accurate and therefore more useful guide as to how hard our money was working.

The Greater our Rate of Stock-turn, the Harder our Money is Working

This principle is most important, for it means that an efficient owner with small capital investment in stock can make as much profit as a less efficient one with larger capital, *if*, and this is imperative, the percentage gross profit does not fall more than to offset the gains resulting from holding smaller stocks. Naturally, if the stock is being turned over more quickly, but the gross percentage is reduced through sacrifice of quantity-buying discounts, the total gross profit might fall. There are many influences involved, and the topic is not a simple one: we have to consider such factors as the greater risk of loss through stock deterioration if larger stocks are held, the greater interest charges to be paid by the retailer who carries heavy stocks bought on borrowed money, the higher discounts usually obtained on quantity buying, loss of sales through over-stocking some lines and so not being able to carry other saleable goods (total capital being limited), and so forth.

It is most unlikely that we can have both maximum gross profit percentage and minimum stock; if you buy in smaller amounts your gross percentage will tend to be lower than if you take advantage of bonus parcels or discount offers. The problem is how to strike a sensible and profitable balance between more stock-turns at a lower gross percentage, and fewer stock-turns at a higher margin. Gross percentage profit is normally calculated on the retail, not on the cost price of an article, i.e. if we buy something for 10p and sell it for 15p our gross percentage profit is usually described as $33\frac{1}{3}\%$, that is 5p on 15p.

Retailers sometimes forget that, provided they are never out of stock of an item, they can often give as good service with a dozen in stock as with a gross. Why carry a spare eleven dozen if this means you are out of stock of an additional saleable line which you could have if your money were not locked up in this excess eleven dozen?

Remember that it is variety of stock, not the amount of stock, which broadly governs your sales. This is always provided you do not allow yourself to run out of lines your customers demand and do not give the impression, often bad psychologically, of having very scanty stocks. There are certain types of merchandise where it is good psychologically for customers to know that you carry small *fresh* stocks. Very often a certain minimum stock is needed for display purposes.

What I have just stated brings us to the basic principle that:—

Stock Variety, not Stock Quantity, gives Sales Volume

YOUR NOTES:-

Chapter 2

CAPITAL and STOCK

Another basic principle:-
What we Buy depends on what we can Sell, or on what we believe we can Sell, at a Profit.

The first rule for successful stock control and buying is therefore that we should study, as fully as possible, our sales prospects. We must do everything we can to know our current and our potential market, our customers, their likes and dislikes (past, present and future), and their spending power.

Let us think of a shop, one we believe is capable of *maximum* sales at present of £200,000 per annum. Let us further assume that we have sufficient money to be able to invest in stock the full amount we think we can profitably employ.

Practical business affairs are not as tidy as our example suggests. Nevertheless, whether we are opening a new shop or taking over an established one, we should have at least some idea of what sales we can reasonably expect. When we buy a shop as a going concern we will normally have records of past results to guide us. If we have bought the stock of the previous owner of the shop we have the disadvantage of not being able to start from scratch, but the advantage of knowing what he believed (rightly or wrongly) was a well-balanced stock; that is, we acquire some market knowledge.

Here we are then, with sales of £200,000 per year (at retail prices) in our hopes, and capital for whatever stock investment we think wise. If we are buying an existing shop we need to decide whether the stock is to be adjusted to suit our own policy.

First work out what the approximate cost would be of goods to sell at £200,000 retail. Your knowledge of the trade, trade price lists, the records of

169

the person you have bought from, official statistics, all these can help. If the cost of the goods is £160,000, a stock of £40,000 will have to be "turned over" four times a year, that is £160,000 divided by £40,000. Should some goods turn over less than four times a year, others must exceed four, but on the whole you need to reach four stock turns per year. A £20,000 stock would call for eight turnovers, an £80,000 stock for two, and so on.

No mistake must be made about the policy. What we are to aim at is the highest possible profit from sales of £200,000 per annum at retail. We must weigh up discount parcels with say an extra 5% gross profit, against a heavier stock with its many drawbacks. Something has to be sacrificed; either the rate of stock turn *or* extra discounts must normally be lost. Remember that maximum sales are, we think, £200,000.

Each shopkeeper will need to work out the facts for his own business, the additional percentage gross profit which bulk buying can secure, and the related losses.

We have been considering the retailer with ample capital; remember that if your capital is limited, any increased buying of one product means less of others, and this will influence the variety of goods you can offer and therefore your sales. On the other hand, larger stocks can mean better display and sales of a particular line.

Variety should, however, be the aim, a comprehensive stock of goods the customers expect you to have and also a stock of new products which you think will sell. It is worth emphasising that:—*with limited capital you must make sure you do not miss sales at a gross profit of perhaps 25% to make maybe an extra 5% or 6% gross on a much smaller turnover. If the variety you offer is not sufficient, you will lose customers even for the lines you do stock.*

A few calculations from your own experience might show occasional cases where a fall in turnover and a higher gross percentage profit leaves you better off. But usually rapid stock turn is the best policy, especially if your capital is limited. You should bear in mind the example of large successful businesses and should not forget the dangers of over-stocking.

Retailers calculate net profit, as a rule, as a percentage of their sales; this is important and necessary information but it is useful to go further and to work out the net profit as a percentage of the total money invested in the business.

As a general rule, if your capital is limited, your wisest plan is to aim at the maximum turnover, but you should work out examples of whether higher turnover at lower % gross profit will give a better or worse return than lower sales at a higher % gross margin.

Retailers should say to themselves "this is the minimum income I seek from my business; how can I most effectively reach it; is my best plan higher sales at low margins or smaller sales at higher percentages?" Each owner of a shop must work out his own policy, according to capital and other resources available.

We must decide on our aim. Most retailers strive to increase their turnover to the maximum and think in terms of sales rather than directly in terms of profit; often this is a fairly safe practical attitude to take, as profits tend to increase with sales, but each shop will have what we can call an "optimum" turnover, which may differ from the "maximum" turnover. The optimum turnover is where the profit is highest, the maximum turnover where the sales are greatest.

Many shops fall far short of their highest possible sales and the general experience is that larger sales mean greater cash profits. The business man should be very alert to notice any *costs* necessary to increase sales; he should always be seeking information on how much additional gross, net, and pure profit, result from growth in turnover.

There are three main stages in the development of a shop. A shop you buy as a "going concern", one you have not yourself started, could be at any one of these stages:—

STAGE 1:—This stage is that during which the owner is making less than he could earn by working as a manager in a similar shop and investing his money.

This stage is the building up or development phase, and it may last only a very brief time or many months. If you can open a shop and *immediately* take enough to cover *all* your costs and show you a pure profit, then you escape Stage 1. Some businesses never pass Stage 1, and the owner is always working for less than he could earn (by his labour and by investing his money), without being an owner himself.

STAGE 2:—Here you are able to add to your sales without proportionally adding to your costs. Many of your larger overheads, such as rates, rent, and to some extent wages, are stationary, at any rate for a period, or are not growing as rapidly, relatively, as your sales; you might for example double your turnover without doubling your wages. Hence in Stage 2 you are at a particularly profitable phase of the shop, and this stage ends when you reach your "optimum" turnover.

STAGE 3:—Now you can only further expand sales by adding substantially to your current expenses and capital investment. You may need for example to make alterations to your premises or take new ones, add highly-paid staff, and so on, if you are to grow further.

This is the stage which *begins* when you have reached your optimum or most profitable turnover as referred to in Stage 2. You now find that unless you change your business "set up" the cost of obtaining further sales makes them unprofitable or even a source of loss.

Suppose that you decide to enlarge your premises or to buy new ones, to go out for the higher potential turnover beyond your present optimum. You might now have to start again at Stage 1, and will pass, if things go well, to Stages 2 and 3 once more. But everything is on a larger scale in this second cycle of events. Once more you may possibly reach Stage 3 and then have to decide again for or against still another cycle in the effort to continue growth.

In every expanding business you come at intervals to these stages; you have to decide periodically whether you are prepared to risk smaller profits over a period, with a view to more than recouping yourself later on.

TOTAL MONEY INVESTED IN A BUSINESS at any time is what the business would sell for at that time, i.e. in the current market.

To assess your investment you must therefore know the present value of lease and goodwill, of fixtures, fittings etc., of stock. It can be very seriously misleading for you to use the figures for which you bought any assets; you need to know *current* values. Goodwill values, for instance, are highly sensitive to market conditions, and can change rapidly.

If you own the freehold of the premises from which you operate your business you should take specialist advice on what would be a current economic rental for the premises or for the part used for business. This information could then be taken into reckoning by the valuer assessing your goodwill. A specialist valuer could advise you on the point of an economic rent and could place a value on goodwill etc., in the current market. Market knowledge, up to date knowledge, is necessary, so consult your valuer.

YOUR NOTES:-

Chapter 3

DANGERS OF OVER-STOCKING

Give much thought to the dangers of over-stocking, but keep a sense of balance; the following points should be kept steadfastly in mind:—

1. The customer is your first consideration; offer a representative stock and give a good service.

2. To place frequent small orders and check numerous deliveries *adds* to your running costs.

3. When prices are rising, stocks could be kept higher than under normal conditions. However, buying goods in abnormal quantities because of expected price changes, is speculation, and speculation is not a normal part of retail business.

4. It is vital to remember, in the enthusiasm of trying to guard against over-stocking, that sales must not be sacrificed; missed sales mean money lost at the time, and can also cause prolonged damage to the goodwill of the business.

5. A bad impression is given if the public see empty-looking shelves, windows, and shop. It is unwise to keep stock so low that you cannot give effective display and that people conclude you must be very short of capital.

6. Regulate the amount of your stock to the type of business, to sales (actual and potential), and to your capital position.

After these opening comments, I emphasise that to carry "surplus" stock means to reduce your profit, directly and indirectly.

You reduce your profit directly, because you have money lying idle or not bringing in the highest return it could show. You are reducing profit indirectly, because surplus stock has unfortunate effects on your customers and goodwill, this in turn reducing your trade and profit.

Here are some of the bad effects of carrying surplus stock (for a definition of surplus stock please see ahead):—

If you have surplus stock your shop is carrying goods in store longer than is necessary. If you do this you are usually increasing the chance of deterioration or that items will go out of fashion; but stocks such as antiques and some wines can grow in value as time goes by.

If you sell goods not perfect in quality or condition you will certainly lose customers, and legal action might be taken against you.

Should you avoid the serious error of selling imperfect goods (unless, of course, they can legally be sold and furthermore they are offered and described as imperfect), you will either have to reduce their price or write them off completely. Any reduction in price or complete "writing-off" can soon wipe out the profit on the "non-surplus" part of the stock of the goods concerned.

For example, if you buy one hundred items at £1.50 each to sell at £2.25 each, your gross profit on selling the whole batch would be £75.00. Suppose that you sell eighty and have to write off twenty; then your gross profit on the deal is eighty times £2.25 (£180.00) minus one hundred times £1.50 (£150.00) = £30.00.

The failure to sell *one fifth* of the goods has reduced by *three fifths* the gross profit, which is £30.00 instead of £75.00. The position becomes even more serious when profit margins are lower and when a larger part of the goods is left unsold on your shelves.

If, with the above goods, thirty were unsold, our gross profit would be seventy times £2.25 (£157.50) minus one hundred times £1.50 (£150.00) = £7.50. Failure to sell *thirty per cent* of the goods has reduced our gross profit by *ninety* per cent (from £75.00 to £7.50).

Finally, take an example where the gross margin is lower than in the previous cases. Suppose that we buy 100 items at £1.50 each, to retail at £2.00 each, and that thirty are unsold and written off.

The cost of the 100 items is £150.00 and the money received for them is 70 times £2.00 or £140. We have made a loss (gross) of £10 instead of an expected gross profit of £50.

I have emphasised, as it deserves, the point I am making, and enough should now have been said to show how dangerous it is to buy so many of an article that some remain unsold. You could work out a table to meet your own case, showing the effect of varying portions of goods being unsold at different gross percentage profits. A transaction can very easily prove unprofitable if we do not sell, completely and at their normal retail price, the goods we have bought.

Remember that in our examples we have been considering only *gross* profit. There could hardly fail to be a very heavy *net loss* in our third example.

If you are in any doubt, buy smaller quantities and sell out a line entirely, rather than heavier quantities with a discount but with the prospect of unsold "remainders".

Idle goods on your shelves are eating up your money. Consider a parcel of goods which has cost you £3.75 (selling at £5, to show you 25% gross profit on the retail price), and which should turn over four times per year. If the goods sell as normally expected, you would therefore make £1.25 gross profit every three months, that is £5 per year, if you re-order each time you sell out (or, in practice, just before you sell out).

If these goods do not sell, then every three months they remain on your shelf, they are costing you £1.25 lost gross profit. They are not merely failing to contribute to your overheads, but apart from not making the £1.25 they should, these goods are occupying space, have to be counted, insured, dusted, and so on. This merchandise is a source of net loss to you.

One of these £3.75 parcels remaining on your shelf for nine months (during which the money invested in the goods should have turned over three times and should have earned £3.75 gross profit), has in reality lost you £3.75, that is the original cost price (or more if you bring in the points of the previous paragraph). If, at long last, the goods sell for something above their cost price, this can be set against the loss of gross profit; goods of this type are, however, more likely to be sold, if they are sold at all, at less than they cost you. Here again, examples applicable to your own business could be worked out to give a clear picture of what gross profit is lost when various proportions of goods showing varying gross profits remain unsold for different periods of time.

In the foregoing I have left out of my reckoning what the money, had it been *reinvested* in stock, could earn for us; this matter of reinvestment is described later. I have assumed that if you had not tied up your £3.75 in the goods concerned, you could have bought other goods instead which would have sold at 25% gross profit on retail price, and which would have turned over every three months.

You might say that, had you not invested £3.75 in the unsaleable goods, you would not have spent this money on stock. In that case you could very well have been receiving interest on your money and you could presumably at any rate have avoided losing it completely; or you may have some other business use for the cash, to bring you in a fair return.

If you have been *borrowing* to purchase the stock, then you have no doubt been paying interest to enable you to buy something which loses you money.

Everyone holding goods for resale must make some mistakes; this is one of the risks you take in business. The profit you make from your shop is the reward for risk bearing, but the risk should be kept down when possible. You should realise just how much money dead stock costs you and how important it is to turn over your cash held in the form of stock.

Changes in retail selling prices increase the risk of carrying larger stocks than you need.

The changes can work either way and the value of stock might increase or decrease as a result. The shopkeeper who buys extra amounts of stock because he expects price rises, can fairly argue that he is serving his customers well, and helping his goodwill, if he can manage to sell at current prices for a longer time than otherwise.

Many retailers, in times of rising prices, stock up in order to increase their profit. Such action is speculation, rather than normal business, and should the market change, big losses can follow instead of "windfall" gains.

A study of speculation does not come within the subject of normal trading, and I leave the topic with the advice: make a clear distinction in your business between speculation, which *increases* risk, and ordinary business where you try to keep risk to a minimum for the type of trade you are in. If your capital is fairly limited, a *normal* business risk, with a *normal* chance of profit, is sounder than gambling on exceptional price changes and possibility of unusually high profit. Always remember that speculation involves the risk of heavy losses as well as of heavy gains.

Fashions change; you should be doubly chary of holding large stocks of fashion merchandise. Very often with these goods, the bigger your stock and display, the less you sell. Many of us like to think we are buying something a little scarce, something not being sold to all and sundry; conversely, some people like to feel they are buying what "everyone is buying". You must sum up the psychology of your own trade and customers.

Large stocks require more storage space; space is money, as it means lighting, rent, rates, heating, and so forth.

The greater the variety you offer in goods suitable to your trade, the more profit you should make.

You may wish to sell your shop. If you do, your main assets will usually be lease and goodwill, stock, and fixtures and fittings, etc. Or you may have the freehold to sell instead of transferring a lease.

A business may take a long time to sell, or even fail to sell, because the stock is too heavy in relation to the profits. With over-stocking, the capital a purchaser requires can be so great that the number of possible buyers is very much reduced. Furthermore, the investment is less attractive as the percentage yield on the capital is lower.

It is very difficult to reduce stock to suit a buyer, even if you are willing to do so. In any event, unless you have another similar shop to absorb the goods, what are you to do with any stock a purchaser would not take? It can be a

179

complicated matter to agree with a prospective buyer on *what* goods should be removed by you to bring the total price down to what he can or is prepared to spend.

It is worth repetition that it is normally *variety* of goods, not large stocks with limited assortment, which brings sales volume.

Chapter 4

KNOW YOUR MARKET

The aims of stock control can be classified as

Offensive and Defensive

By Offensive control I mean the type based on the intention to find out what additional products could profitably be added to the range already stocked. This is expansion control, aggressive and dynamic, and involves the most full and careful market research.

By Defensive control I mean the kind mainly concerned with making sure you do not run out of stock of the lines you normally carry. This is vital if you are to maintain the goodwill of your customers, but it is not likely to increase your turnover so rapidly as well-designed Offensive activity.

An efficiently managed shop should use both types of control referred to; defensive control is essential for every business, while offensive control is necessary for all seeking continually growing trade. We all lose some customers for reasons beyond our control, so unless we constantly find new ones and/or sell more to existing ones our business will go into decline.

Market Research can be roughly divided into two main sections. These two we can call **Desk** research and **Field** research.

1. *DESK RESEARCH.* This you can carry out inside your business. You use the data from the internal records you yourself make, from the accounts, from sales records, from lists of credit customers, from notes of complaints received or of praise, from notes of special requests from customers, etc. Add to this the information you can collect from outside sources such as trade papers, interfirm comparisons (please see ahead), government publications, etc.

2. *FIELD RESEARCH.* This is research about market conditions etc. in your own shopping area or potential area, that is the area you serve or could serve. You or your staff could do much of this work, or you could employ outside specialists.

Be careful not to look narrowly at your area. If for instance you are considering addition of a mail order outlet for your merchandise the whole world could be your prospective market. Remember that mail-order business has its own special difficulties as well as its own attractions and that industrious forethought and planning is something you cannot do without if you are to succeed.

Some forms of market research might be regarded as having an advertising aspect. This is fine if such advertising does not offend any code of ethics you might be committed to. If you have any doubts, find out *first*. In some types of activity advertising is looked upon as unethical.

Information you collect from these two main kinds of research must be as factual and as specific as possible. You must relate the information to your own shop or shops, must study it with an expert eye. Any unpleasant truths which are unearthed must be faced and dealt with; don't reject data just because you don't like it.

I recommend you to prepare a self-questionnaire on the following lines and that you open files of data on the matters referred to, as necessary. Ask yourself:—

What is my drawing area?   (see maps in file —)

What is the population?
    within half a mile? . . . .
    within one mile? . . . .
    within X miles? . . . .

What is the population trend?
    growing? . . . .
    falling? . . . .

What is the population composition?
how many teenagers? ....
how many pensioners?, etc. ....
and the trend? .... (see file —)
what is their work and income? ....

Have I studied the local and other appropriate development plans?
when? ....
where? ....
N.B. You might need to study plans for other areas affecting yours.

Have I a panel of customers to consult?
When started? ....
When met? .... Give dates .... (see file —)

Additional products and services
What have customers asked for? .... (see file —)
What action have I taken? .... (see file —)

Complaints
Received from customers about my service etc. .... (see file —)
Received about facilities in the area generally. .... (see file —)
Do I note what family and friends say about this?

Competitors
When did I last carry out any observation?
Date .... (see file —)

Analysis of passers by

    Date   . . . .

    Date   . . . .

    Date   . . . .

(see file —)

These are of course only suggested questions; every shop is unique, with its own individual angles, so make out your own questionnaire.

NOTE: Interfirm Comparison Schemes

If you take part in one of these you supply to the organisers [perhaps a trade body], in confidence, details of your turnover, wages, floor space, rent, rates, etc., etc. You and others taking part receive from the organisers summarised information on businesses similar to your own (you are not given the identity of individual shops). To compare your own figures with others in similar circumstances can be revealing.

Chapter 5

BUDGETARY CONTROL AND BUYING

From investigations made as suggested in Chapter 4 you should be able to form a *fairly close estimate* of what sales your shop is capable of making, over the next year or other period, *provided you carry the requisite stock.*

Remember that the sales forecast can only be an estimate, but you should find year by year that your accuracy increases and that actual sales come closer and closer to the forecast you have made.

It is important to realise that you are bound to make some mistakes, through events within or beyond your own control. For instance it is not possible to forecast what legislation can come into force and upset your calculations, nor can you, at the present time, know accurately what the weather is going to be.

If you persistently attempt to analyse the market, your knowledge will improve all the time. So do not be unduly discouraged if your first forecast is quite wide of the actual results, but try to find out where and why you have failed.

Any carefully worked out forecast, taking into account past results and future prospects as you assess them, is better than no forecast at all.

The sales forecast is the first step, the basic and essential one, in starting a system of budget control; from this forecast everything else grows.

Let us agree, for simplicity of calculation, that you have made your forecast and estimate that, in your next trading year, you should be able to make sales of £200,000 at retail prices.

We will also assume, for the moment, that you aim to end the year with about the same value of goods in stock as at the beginning.

We now have something to work on. From our assumptions, you will obviously need to *buy*, over the year, goods to retail at £200,000. You know your expected approximate gross profit margin, and if this is say 25% (again an easy figure for calculation), you will buy goods costing £150,000. I have employed the usual procedure of taking the gross percentage profit as being on the price at which we sell our goods.

You should keep a constant check on the value, at *cost*, of the orders you place, and your *average* monthly purchases should be £12,500 (i.e. £150,000 divided by 12). You need to keep a continuous day to day record of the value at cost price of orders you have placed, and at any time therefore you should know how much has been spent of your monthly £12,500. If in one month you overspend, a corresponding reduction will have to be made later; on the other hand, if you do not buy your full quota of goods one month you will be able to buy more afterwards.

If your sales fluctuate a great deal you will require to make your forecast and purchases on this basis. Usually, but not always, purchases will be made just ahead of the expected corresponding sales, and will vary in line with them.

Naturally you will watch your sales carefully, to see how closely they are in accord with your forecast, and if you find that they are heavily down or up you will adjust your buying plan accordingly. It is important that you govern the system, and that you do not let the system control you. Sales and purchases must constantly be reviewed and compared with the forecast, so you need to be both flexible and practical.

By using this very simple method you are able to ensure that you are not under- or over-buying to any important extent. I stress that we are not expecting to be absolutely accurate, as this is neither possible nor necessary. What we are doing is keeping stock under control without more than a few minutes' daily work to keep the system going. Your sales you already know from your normal cashing-up and cash register reading. Purchases you can record in your order book or books, by noting the *cost* of goods ordered, or you can extract the figures from invoices.

Which method you use for noting purchases will depend on your circumstances. If you record as you place an order (a copy of every order should always be kept), you are as up to the minute as you can be. There is

SALES AND PURCHASES FOR THE YEAR

JANUARY 1st, 19____ to DECEMBER 31st, 19____

Estimated total sales £200,000

Estimated total purchases £150,000

	SALES				PURCHASES			
	Estimated	Running Total £	*Actual*	Running Total £	*Estimated*	Running Total £	*Actual*	Running Total £
J	10,000	10,000			12,000	12,000		
F	15,000	25,000			12,000	24,000		
M	15,000	40,000			12,500	36,500		
A	15,000	55,000			13,500	50,000		
M	20,000	75,000			13,500	63,500		
J	20,000	95,000			15,000	78,500		
J	25,000	120,000			14,000	92,500		
A	25,000	145,000			13,000	105,500		
S	20,000	165,000			10,000	115,500		
O	15,000	180,000			11,000	126,500		
N	10,000	190,000			11,500	138,000		
D	10,000	200,000			12,000	150,000		
	200,000	200,000			150,000	150,000		

N.B.:— Purchases are shown against the month in which the goods are ordered, although delivery may be later and payment for them later still.

bound to be some time gap between the order and the invoice, but the latter will show any goods not sent from your order, will indicate settlement or other discounts, etc., and give you a more accurate figure. Probably your best plan is to record purchases in both ways, that is by having a running total in your order book or order books and then checking this against invoices as these are received later on.

It is worth repeating, for emphasis, that a copy of all orders must be kept. Orders must be confirmed *in writing*. Without strict obedience to this rule your system will break down.

As I have said, a few minutes' work each day will keep your control system in action. Once you have made your forecast and buying budget, the rest follows naturally. You will quickly notice any trends of business which need immediate action, and you will have closer control and fuller knowledge than can be possible without a system.

If you are computerised, an appropriate programme will reduce the already small amount of time needed.

At the end of this chapter I list some advantages of a simple budgetary control plan as described. Remember that the starting point is the market investigation and sales forecast; carrying this out will be of immense value to you in conducting your shop, quite apart from its place in the budgetary control system.

The method I put forward has been kept free from unnecessary complications. It can, however, be readily made more embracing to suit individual needs or wishes.

A word of warning here. It is so very easy to collect figures and never use them that I suggest you make quite sure what information you must have and will act on. It you want facts for their own sake or general knowledge, and not strictly for their direct usefulness in your business, that is for you to decide. The following elaborations are often of great *practical* value, but I recommend you to gather only information which you seriously mean to employ.

Here are a few ways in which the scope of our system can be widened; it is for you to decide on other variations to meet your own needs.

1. The sales forecast can be sub-divided between different classes of merchandise, and the purchasing budget split up in the same way.

For example, a sweets and tobacco shop could have further columns in the chart so that separate monthly sales and purchase *estimates* and *actual* figures are given for tobacco and for sweets.

Again, a pharmacist might decide on separate analysed figures for dispensing, cosmetics, photographics, etc.

Clearly our chart could quickly become very complex. Sub-divisions of the type mentioned would need to be linked up with the cash register or computer or other systems of recording and analysing sales, and similarly you would need to classify your purchases.

A simple system which is up to date and acted upon promptly is better than a more ambitious one which might be giving facts you cannot easily digest and use.

2. You could, instead of classifying your goods into types of merchandise, sub-divide sales and purchases according to the gross profit on the items concerned.

For example, sales of goods showing 20% to 25% gross could be separately noted from merchandise showing 30% to 35%, and so on. This system is not easy to operate, but it can be helpful in keeping a running check on profits. Here I must remind you that no check on profits can be accurate unless accurate valuations of stock, from physical recordings, are carried out at the beginning *and* at the end of the period being checked.

3. You can use the system to forecast what payments you will need to make, and when, for the goods you propose to order. You can then if necessary make special financial arrangements to meet the accounts. It is much wiser to make such arrangements well before you might need extra money, for example on a bank overdraft. It is advantageous to go in advance with a clear and logical case to place before the Bank, rather than to find yourself suddenly short of fluid capital.

Some advantages of a Budgetary Control System

1. You first of all make a sales forecast; to do this is in itself of value as it means that you need to investigate your market and your potential market. Your forecast should not be just a guess. You should draw on the knowledge and experience of staff as well as using any help you can get outside the business. You could find it valuable to bring in a consultant.

2. Purchases and sales are constantly kept in reasonable balance.

3. Following from (2), you will be able to keep your stock under control. The amount of stock will vary according to the plan you have made, and not "willy-nilly".

4. You will know approximately what your cash position is likely to be at future dates. This will help you to handle private and business problems more efficiently. For example your holiday could be arranged for a time when you have plenty of cash in the Bank, or for when business is expected to be fairly quiet.

5. You have a sales target to aim for. You can, with the appropriate record system, see whether any section of goods is falling behind schedule, and you can take any steps possible to remedy this or to switch your efforts into other channels.

6. You will improve your relationships with people giving financial or other help if you can show them that you are controlling your business in a planned and methodical way.

The foregoing are just some of the general benefits from a budgetary control plan; you will probably, as you proceed, find many more advantages.

The present outline of a budgetary control system is directed mainly to the *stock* aspects of such a system. A *full* budgetary control system starts with the sales forecast, but it will take into account all actual and expected receipts and outgoings of the business, and not only sales and purchases; capital as well as revenue items will be included.

A full budgetary control system will show purchases, wages, rates, rent, in fact all expected payments which have to be made during the period covered by the budget, as well as all expected receipts from sales, rents, and so forth. Such a budget will enable you to forecast what your approximate financial position will be at any time during the year or other period ahead for which the budget is prepared, and the approximate profit you should make. Full description of such a system is not within the scope of this book, but there is plenty of literature on the subject.

Retailers are recommended to learn at least the elements of budgetary control. Such knowledge will be a powerful help in conducting any business and will increase one's breadth of business outlook.

A budget or control plan enables you, by preparing for any problem well in advance, to avoid or reduce financial danger; the smaller shopkeeper is urged to study the idea in helping increase his competitiveness against larger rivals. I end this chapter by stressing yet again that *the system begins with a sales forecast* based on a careful study of your actual and potential market.

YOUR NOTES:-

Chapter 6

GROSS PROFIT VARIATIONS

It is the net profit figure which draws the eye of most people when a profit and loss account is handed to them. This is perhaps natural, and net profit has an importance which hardly needs stressing. Gross profit percentages reveal more, and are often more significant, than is however realised. These gross margins well repay constant and close study.

The gross profit percentage of a retail business varies for one or more of many reasons. It is useful to group by type the factors which cause these fluctuations. Some changes are natural, following logically from the policy of the owner; others are the result of legislation or other external forces beyond his or her direct control. A third type embraces changes due to human frailty or error and is closely related to a fourth category of variation which is the outcome of faulty business records. How we make up our groups for the purpose of study does not matter a great deal; the vital point is that we should be gross profit conscious.

It is not enough to think that all is well if the gross profit in our shop varies only slightly from year to year. Stability *or* fluctuation can each be the symptom of something wrong, and neither should be taken for granted.

Let us now define the four groups already referred to. The categories we use are not rigid, and there is some overlapping from one section to another.

A.   NATURAL VARIATIONS, due to:

(1)   *Changes in the character of the business.* These changes might be due to internal or external influences. The decision of the owner to add a new department or speciality, or to start new trading methods such as say part-payment terms for expensive items, must have an effect on profit margins. As an example of outside influence we could take the building of a factory in or near a district which had hitherto been almost entirely residential; this could

well mean a demand for products which had not previously been handled.

(2) *Changes in buying policy*. A decision to try and run the business on smaller stocks, or conversely to take up more bonus parcels, must obviously affect the gross margin.

(3) *Changes in the sales policy*. The raising or lowering of prices asked for such goods as packed lines or "own-name" products will be reflected in the gross profit.

(4) *The opening or closing of a branch*. Such a move is bound to have repercussions on the gross profits produced. Buying will doubtless be either cut down or stepped up and margins will vary accordingly.

(5) *Increase or fall in the turnover*. A change in the fortunes of the business will make more profitable buying possible or may on the other hand mean smaller orders and reduced percentages.

(6) *Stock deterioration*. Everyone in business makes some bad buys; every buyer finds he has some goods which have fallen in value. Changes in fashion, chemical or biological action, and other factors, take their toll of the profits made. As against this, we occasionally have a rise in stock values through economic conditions.

B.   VARIATIONS DUE TO LEGISLATION, etc. (outside influences):

(1) *Price changes* by manufacturers often bring a variation in the gross margin. The margin on goods which are already in stock may be affected and the shop carrying large stocks will stand to gain or lose more than the small concern.

(2) *V.A.T.* If the gross percentage is calculated on the V.A.T. inclusive sales, changes in V.A.T. rates will affect the result. The V.A.T. exclusive figures should therefore be used in the calculation.

(3) *Price cutting*. If a retailer has to reduce the price of certain goods to compete with price cutting activities in the area, the gross margin will clearly

fall. Should the decision be not to accept lower prices but to stop handling the goods in question, then the outcome could be a higher gross profit, as very often the lines which are cut do not show a high margin even on the normal selling price.

(4) *National monetary policy.* This is outside the control of any individual owner. Government policy on such matters as credit and interest rates can play havoc with any retailer's plans.

C. LEAKAGES, IN GOODS AND/OR IN MONEY:

(1) *Shoplifting* is most difficult to assess. Some businesses are hardly affected, while others must have serious losses. There is little need to do more than mention shoplifting as an influence which depresses the profit margin. Large scale and noticeable theft, for example by breaking and entering, is a different matter, being normally covered by insurance as is damage by fire, etc.

(2) *Damage to stock* through breakage or soiling is part of the risk taken by anyone carrying goods on his shelves. The dropped bottle of perfume, the sponge which has become dirty, the chocolate which has deteriorated through undue heat or cold, means yet another drain on the gross margin.

(3) *Wrong prices* charged to customers. The general tendency here is only too clearly for gross profit to be lowered. Any overcharging is in most cases quickly pointed out by the buyer, while often the undercharge tends to be "forgotten" or "not noticed".

(4) *Inaccurate weighing*, counting or measuring. Here, as with incorrect prices, the bias is against the retailer and his gross margin. The customer seldom fails to draw attention to any shortage.

D. FAULTY RECORDS OF SALES, PURCHASES AND STOCK:

If we remind ourselves briefly of the four basic figures needed in the calculation of our gross profit we shall throw into bold relief the importance of accurate records. Gross profit is, we remember, the difference between the total of—

Sales at retail price plus closing stock at our year end, and the total of—

Purchases at cost plus opening stock.

Stock in each case to be at cost. From this it naturally follows that if any one of the four basic figures is incorrect no reliance can be placed on the gross profit computed.

It bears repeating—that to arrive at an accurate gross profit figure, we must have accurate figures for OPENING STOCK, for CLOSING STOCK, for SALES, and for PURCHASES.

(1)   It is still not always realised that an inaccurate stock figure affects two years' accounts (except, of course, in the case of the opening stock in a new or newly acquired business). From the formula we have given for calculating the gross profit, it is clear that if the stock at the end of any year is overvalued then the gross profit must be overstated to the same extent. But the closing stock for one year is the opening stock for the next, and our formula will show that if the opening stock is overstated by £XXXX, the gross profit for the year concerned will be shown as £XXXX less than the true figure. Not until accurate stock figures are available for both the beginning *and* the end of a year can a correct gross profit figure result, and we must also have correct purchases and sales figures. Elementary maybe, but frequently overlooked.

(2)   *Outstandings*. From our previous remarks and the formula for gross profit we can see that if goods are taken into stock in one financial year but are invoiced in the *next* financial year as purchases, we are bound to miscalculate the gross profit for both the years involved. Similarly, inaccuracy will follow if goods are invoiced and treated as having been received in one financial year but have not been taken into that year's stock figure.

The errors we have just described spring from incorrect recording of goods around the end of a financial year, and we have probably said enough to draw attention to the importance of making sure that purchases are allocated to the appropriate year.

The term "outstandings" means in this context, goods which have been taken into stock in one year but not invoiced therein; it is not a question of whether the goods have been paid for in the year they were received, but of correctly recording purchases and stock. It should be readily inferred that it is, by the same arguments, imperative that sales should also be allocated to the appropriate financial year. Special care should be taken with goods on "Sale or Return".

(3) *Invoices*. Any laxity in the checking of prices, quantities, and totals, will result in some error in the working out of the gross profit.

(4) *Credit Sales*. Any failure to charge up to a customer, goods supplied on a credit account, means a loss. The point is an obvious one but is referred to as it is so easy to forget, in a busy selling spell, to make a note of articles handed over to a customer with an account.

(5) *Inter-branch transfers*. Where two or more shops are involved in the movement of stock from one to the other, a frequent source of error in gross profit figures arises. From the formula given previously we know that any goods supplied to a business "gratis" will inflate the gross margin, while the gross profit of the shop "giving the stock away" as it were, will suffer correspondingly. Should separate accounts for each business not be kept, then failure to record the stock transfers accurately will not affect the overall gross margin, but if the accounts do show individual profit figures, then these will mislead if stock from one branch to another is not recorded just as carefully as purchases from outside suppliers.

(6) *Cash Records*. There is a tendency for some retailers to make odd payments out of the till or cash register. It is vital that any such payments should be carefully noted and allocated. To take money out of the till without a proper record means that the takings are depressed by the amount involved, with resultant inaccuracy in one of the four essential pieces of information for our gross profit calculation.

(7) *Staff Sales*. A careful record should be made of any staff sales made at a discount. It is unlikely that such sales will vary greatly from year to year, and they might well, therefore, be not so much a cause of fluctuation as of a continually lower gross profit margin than one would expect. The effect is usually small in relation to other factors influencing gross margins.

We have given a variety of reasons why the gross profit margin can vary from year to year. Some of the factors referred to will tend to raise the gross margin shown, while others will exert a lowering influence; a third type includes factors which can act either way, according to circumstances. A gross profit which appears "normal" could hide compensating errors, although this is more feasible over short than long periods. It would need a most improbable series of balancing errors for these not to reveal themselves in the long run.

It is more likely that gross profit variations of a *large percentage amount* will occur in the small than in the big concern. Unless there is some grave basic cause of great fluctuation, the various factors are more apt to be fairly consistent from year to year in the larger concern. By the "law of averages", which operates more obviously when large numbers are involved, the chances of things evening themselves out over a period are enhanced in the business with the heavier turn-over. Nevertheless, variations are to be expected in all sizes of shop.

From what we have said, it is only too clear that retail business is very much in the grip of external forces as regards the gross profit margins which can be made.

We cannot tell whether the future will show a rise or a fall in gross margins as a whole; it is I think a safe forecast to say that the signs are of continuing fluctuations. Change, not stability, is what we can expect.

Chapter 7

WHERE AND HOW TO STORE STOCK

The object of buying stock is to sell it at a profit, and we do this by being of service to our customers.

This matter of service means even more than having the right goods at the required time and place at suitable prices. Where and how you store the goods on your premises is part of the skill of keeping shop. What helps you to be efficient will be to your customer's benefit, and what assists her will react to your profit.

The following are points which need careful attention when you plan the storage of your stock.

1. *SPEED OF SERVICE:*—With some lines the customer's main wish is to be in and out of the shop as quickly as possible. See that any such items in your stock are handy for your assistants to sell. You should make certain that you and your staff avoid long walks, with delay for the customer, in fetching the goods or in taking payment.

   Very often these quick selling "pick-up" lines can be kept together; perhaps in some instances they can be kept "pre-wrapped" near the shop entrance.

2. *CONVENIENCE OF STOCK-CHECKING:*—Goods are sometimes stored in groups of similar merchandise, or it might be preferable to store all the goods of one particular manufacturer together.

   Often a satisfactory arrangement is to keep similar and related merchandise in the same part of the shop, with the products of each manufacturer together within the larger group. If this does not fit in with the point under heading No. 1 in this chapter, it could be useful to have some goods stored in two or more places, some for extra-quick service, say on a special counter, and some for normal selling. The arrangement must vary with the type of goods and with each shop according to its size, lay out, etc.

Keeping goods in more than one place makes stock checks more difficult, but the customer must come first.

Keep stock as *visible* as you can, for instance under glass, and also so arranged that counting is easy.

3. *MANY GOODS NEED SPECIAL STORAGE CONDITIONS:*—Some goods must be kept cool, or out of direct sunlight, others might be damaged by too cold conditions, and so on.

Here again we may have to balance advantages and disadvantages of various positions in the shop.

Naturally, *condition* of the goods must take priority over speed of service. It is no use taking a risk of selling goods in bad condition, just for the sake of being able to handle them quickly; the legal aspects, quite apart from the bad effect on goodwill, of selling items which are out of condition, must be kept in mind. Examples are plentiful in the food trade; ice cream, fish, vegetables, and so on. Other examples are many goods stocked by chemists, among them penicillin, hydrogen peroxide and insulin.

4. *LEGAL REQUIREMENTS:*—There are special regulations governing the conditions of storage of many items such as poisons. It is laid down by law, for example, that morphine, cocaine, etc., in a retail pharmacy, must be kept locked up, the key being in the personal possession of a pharmacist. Clearly legal requirements must take precedence over other storage factors, and the immediate convenience of the customer cannot always govern storage. It is in the interests of customers and the general public that dangerous drugs and any goods needing special care in their use should be stored with proper safeguards.

5. *THE SELLING ANGLE:*—There are some articles which a customer wants to inspect at leisure or to discuss in privacy before making a decision on buying. Many goods need to be demonstrated or tried out, for example electric razors. In certain cases it might be desirable or even

essential to provide a room in which the customer can have the seclusion he or she requires; for instance when such goods as surgical appliances, elastic stockings, etc., have to be fitted, or hearing aids are being selected.

6. *THE STAFF POINT OF VIEW:*—A wise proprietor will avoid needless walking or carrying by his staff, and he will, as far as is possible, keep the goods in his shop readily accessible.

Quite apart from the time factor, the safety aspect of storage should be kept in mind. Reduce to a minimum, climbing and stretching out for stock, and make sure that steps and ladders are strong, stable, and well maintained.

In considering these aspects of stock storage, the shopkeeper should think of things from the customer's point of view and also from that of his staff. These points of view coincide, as without staff there is no service, and without customers there is no need for staff.

Your biggest single expense item, after wages and salaries, is almost certainly what your premises cost you in rent, or rent equivalent if the freehold is owned by you, and rates. And rent and rates are what is called "fixed overheads". In these times they are certainly not fixed in *one* direction, upwards, but they are usually only too firmly fixed in that you have to pay them whether business is good or bad.

As space is so costly you would expect retailers to make intensive use of it; especially as effective use of space can assist in the most efficient use also of labour, normally your largest single cost.

So if your shop is on the smaller side, say with a selling area of three or four hundred square feet, it is important that you look most closely into how you use your premises as a whole. Yet the smaller area shops are often the very ones not squeezing every pound of turnover from their expensive investment.

Here is a Practical Exercise
Why not find that tape measure and DO IT NOW?
FIRST   measure your selling area: *width* ....

                                        length ....

                                        height ....

             giving a total VOLUME of .... cubic feet approx.

SECOND   Now measure your stockroom(s)

width................

length ....

height ....

giving a total volume of .... cubic feet.

THIRD   Still in the stockroom, work out approximately the volume of empty space, i.e. space taken by passages etc. Then by deduction from the volume arrived at in the previous step you will have the volume occupied by the stock itself.

FOURTH   Divide the stock volume in the previous paragraph by the *distance* round your selling area, that is twice length plus twice width. If your selling area is not symmetrical it will take a moment more.

The latest calculation will tell you the area, in cross section, a shelf round your selling area would have to provide if the shelf is to hold the volume of stock in your stockroom.

Let's Take an Example:—

Selling area 30 feet by 15 feet by 10 feet, giving *4,500 cubic feet,* and perimeter *90 feet.*

Stock room 15 feet by 10 feet by 10 feet, giving *1,500 cubic feet*

   ,,   ,,   empty space, passages, bench etc. *1,000 cubic feet*

   ,,   ,,   effective stockholding volume *500 cubic feet*

$$\frac{STOCKHOLDING\ VOLUME}{SELLING\ AREA\ PERIMETER}\quad \frac{(500\ cubic\ feet)}{(90\ feet)}$$

$$= 5.5\ square\ feet\ approx.$$

From this we see that one shelf say 2 ft. 9 in. from your selling area ceiling and 2 ft. wide, OR 1 ft. 10 in. down and 3 ft. wide, or any combination giving 5.5 square feet approx. cross section, could carry the stock from your stockroom, on the figures taken. Naturally adjustments would be needed to make this example realistic for your particular conditions.

If you carry out this work of measurement and calculation and IF it leads to action, you can achieve at least the following ends:—

A   you can increase the effectiveness of the use of your selling area, by using more of it for storage.

B   You have done (A) without reducing the selling power of your selling area; you have not affected that crucial selling space of a few feet centred on the eye level of your customers.

C   You have made stock control easier and are therefore more likely to be carried out efficiently.

D   You have made stock-handling and replenishment quicker and are therefore making more economical use of your costly staff. You are also making work pleasanter for them, which must be beneficial to you as well.

E   [*AND PROBABLY MOST VALUABLE*], you have freed a stockroom which can become a new department, you have produced an additional floor space of 150 square feet. This is an added third to your original selling area of 450 square feet.

The benefit does not end here, or need not.

Perimeter is crucial, as well as floor space. Perimeter is greater, relatively to floor space, in the smaller areas. A shop ten feet by ten feet, area one hundred square feet, has a perimeter of forty feet; a shop twenty by twenty feet, area four hundred square feet, has perimeter eighty feet; a shop forty by forty feet, area sixteen hundred square feet, gives perimeter one hundred and sixty feet. These figures are of course somewhat reduced by doors etc.

Remember that wall space offers you unobstructed eye level space, and as I have shown, there is relatively more wall space in the small area shop.

Going back to our example, we have added fifty feet wall space to our selling area; our original perimeter was ninety feet, so we have added proportionally much more key *selling* space than we have added actual *floor* space.

When you look at your space from the angle of what sales prospects it offers, as distinct from its mere size, you begin to realise that the big shop does not have everything in its favour.

What if you have no Stock Room? What if you already use your selling area to the full?

Suppose you are restricted above, behind, sideways. There is only one more dimension, assuming that your shop front is fixed as well!

Have you valuable space below, a gold-mine under your feet? Not every business has a cellar or even a few feet empty there below. But if you have, it could be worth a survey, it could be worth finding out whether it can be made dry if it is damp, more accessible if the steps are narrow and tortuous.

It is generally accepted that it is difficult to persuade the public to use stairs, but if you have the kind of space I am describing you might be able to transfer some of your present activities below and thus free space on your ground level. Or could a cellar be *made?*

Before you consider spending a lot of money in alterations, and such work tends to be very costly indeed, you should do three basic things:—

(1)   Undertake *market research* to make as sure as you can that you have potential sales which present lack of space is frustrating.
(2)   Carry out a *cost/benefit* analysis, and a *D.C.F.* [Discounted Cash Flow] estimate.
(3)   Make sure there is no *legal or other bar* to your plans.

Perhaps you consider that you are already getting every possible pound of turnover from your premises, that you could not use them any more effectively than you do? If this is so, I suggest that if you want to expand your business you will have to consider *new* premises.

But very few of us could not, I suggest, find some waste of space in our business. A tape measure and a few sums could pay for this year's holiday and many more to come.

Finally, if you live on the premises, ask yourself whether part or all of the living accommodation could more profitably be used for business.

YOUR NOTES:-

Chapter 8

SURPLUS STOCK

You buy stock with the purpose of selling it at a profit: stock you cannot sell is therefore of no business use. Some stock you might believe you can sell if you persist long enough, but money tied up in such goods for abnormal periods is idle, and often completely lost.

I shall for the present purpose regard as surplus stock, goods which, for any reason, you cannot sell at all, or cannot sell at the normal retail price and at the usual rate for such goods in your shop.

We must be careful here. "Usual" speed of turnover for a particular shop could be once a year, and this might be quite unsatisfactory to most traders. We need to consider the number of weeks' or months' stock of a line as compared with the amount normally held by your *type* of shop. We cannot be dogmatic on the subject.

Goods which have gone out of fashion, or which have deteriorated in quality, are "surplus"; so is part of our stock of any goods which are perfectly saleable as to quality but of which we hold six months' supply where six or four weeks' supply would be adequate. What is surplus stock must, therefore, vary from shop to shop; I shall deal with it according to *why* it is surplus.

The aim is to convert, as far as possible, idle goods into *cash* (which can work for you in a variety of ways), and thereby to help the efficiency of your business. This plan must be carried out at the worst without harming your goodwill, and at the best with real benefit to it.

Here are some ways of dealing with surplus stock:—

1. *Sell the goods to the public at the normal price* and at a speed which will quickly reduce your stock to normal. This quite clearly is not always a helpful suggestion, as presumably you constantly sell as much as you can as quickly

as you can. Nonetheless, it is worth examining your selling methods to see whether some revision is needed.

Efficient selling methods often convert surplus stock into saleable stock. Consider very carefully the selling costs involved.

Note:—When goods will with patience finally sell at regular prices, you have a problem of general stock control rather than the particular one of surplus stock. You should not panic into premature price reduction, neither should you be complacent over goods which are not selling.

2. *Sell the surplus stock to the public at a reduced price.* This can bring difficulties. For example, any "cutting" of products still subject to resale price maintenance could bring trouble from the manufacturer. Furthermore, a "sale" might not be in keeping with your business and it might damage standing and goodwill with the public and suppliers.

3. *Give the surplus goods away.* This could enhance your goodwill if for example you helped some charity by your action, as recipients of the goods might be able to raise money on the articles, or use them. Here again, the makers might be upset and certain lines cannot, in any case, be dealt with in this way. The goods might be poisonous or corrosive or otherwise dangerous, and subject to restrictions on the way in which they can be disposed of.

4. *Destroy the articles*; this is sometimes a good solution, although drastic; it cannot always be done quite as simply as one might expect.

Just as there is the problem of disposing of the waste from atomic power stations, so, on a smaller scale, the disposal of dangerous goods is often difficult, for legal or other reasons.

An interesting case is that of morphine, cocaine, and other drugs which have to be recorded at all stages of their manufacture and distribution, and Home Office authority is needed for their destruction.

5. *Return the goods to the supplier,* for credit at full or part of cost price. This is a very useful solution if it can be achieved.

Normally a supplier prefers to replace the items with other goods rather than to refund cash or issue a credit note. The retailer should avoid being so eager to return unwanted goods that he takes in exchange items which in their turn will present another problem of unsaleability. It may be better policy to accept credit for part of the value of the goods, this credit to be used in buying articles of your own choice, rather than to have full credit in the form of goods selected by the supplier.

Remember always that your aim is to make more money or good selling stock available for your business, and let this general principle guide you in your decision. Five pounds' worth of saleable goods are worth more than an abundance of "shelf-warmers".

Retailers are often reluctant to approach a supplier with a request for help over a stock difficulty. There must be give and take, and it is not to the benefit of a manufacturer to have a retailer stocked-up with goods he cannot sell. While the over-stock remains, and perhaps afterwards, the retailer is not a good customer for the manufacturer concerned. The problem is a mutual one, and so should be faced together.

The more valuable or potentially valuable a retailer's account and goodwill are to a manufacturer, the greater the effort will the latter make to assist. In deciding on the merits of any proposal made to him, the retailer should bear in mind what I say elsewhere on the cost, in terms of lost profit, of holding unnecessary stocks.

6. *Co-operate with other retailers in placing surplus stock*. With some articles it might be found that no sales are made in one part of a district, while in another business quite near at hand they are selling well. There is, therefore, much to be said for local schemes whereby retailers in a trade arrange to let one another know, perhaps through their trade organisation, of surpluses they hold.

Mr. Jones, for example, with too much of product Y, might very well have a mutually profitable deal with Mr. Smith who has too much of product A, provided each retailer has a market for the goods his colleague cannot sell.

7. *Hold on to the surplus goods* in the hope that sooner or later they will sell. What this can cost you in money is dealt with elsewhere, but other costs are also involved.

Customers have a way of sensing when goods are old, even if they are not glaringly so. Your name suffers if this impression of old stock is given, unless you happen to deal in antiques! The policy of "holding-on" is not to be recommended unless you have concrete reasons for believing you can in the end sell safely and profitably.

8. *Offer to dealers in surplus stocks.* In some trades there are specialist dealers who buy and sell surplus stock of various types; often such dealers are ready to make quick offers and speedily relieve the vendor of the goods. It is probably fair to say that, in general, if a dealer is buying goods for re-sale to another retailer he can afford to pay less than can a retailer who will be selling direct to the public. It does, however, sometimes happen that goods can only be sold through specialist dealers for the trade concerned.

9. *Instruct specialist Valuers and Agents for your trade* to offer on your behalf.

I have in this chapter been dealing mainly with small amounts of surplus stock. Sometimes an entire stock might be for disposal, due for instance to the closing down of a business, and here it is particularly helpful to consult the specialist Valuers and Agents referred to under (9).

I have made various suggestions for dealing with surplus stock, and advise you to act at once should you decide that certain goods are surplus. The longer you wait, the less your chance of credit or exchange, and the greater the loss you will, in the end, almost certainly suffer.

To follow up what I wrote earlier, shall we now suppose that we have say £200* (at cost price) of surplus stock, and that, through capital shortage, we are not able to stock the full variety of goods we could sell; also let us assume that we normally turn over our stock four times a year and make a gross profit of $33\frac{1}{3}\%$ on cost, i.e. 25% on selling price.

---

* If my definition, earlier in this chapter, of "surplus stock" is used, many businesses are carrying many times this amount surplus.

On these figures the £200, invested in *saleable* stock, could bring us in from extra sales, a gross profit over a year of $4 \times 33\frac{1}{3}\% \times £200 = £267$ approximately; this additional *gross* profit should produce a higher than usual *net* profit, as not all selling expenses go up in proportion to sales.

If the extra *net* profit were left in the business and also invested in fast-selling stock, giving us additional sales, we would make more still on our money as the following example shows:—

January 1st:—£200 extra stock (at cost).

April 1st:—Extra gross profit £67 approximately.
    Extra *net* profit say £40.

The extra *net* profit of £40 is invested in stock, and our total extra stock is now £240 (at cost) (i.e. £200 plus £40).

July 1st:— Extra gross profit £80 (i.e. $33\frac{1}{3}\%$ of £240).
    Extra *net* profit say £48.

The £48 extra *net* profit is invested in stock and our total extra stock over the year so far is now £288 (i.e. £200 plus £40 plus £48) at cost value.

October 1st:— Extra gross profit £96 (i.e. $33\frac{1}{3}\%$ of £288).
    Extra *net* profit say £58.

The extra *net* profit of £58 is invested in stock, and total extra stock over the year so far is now £346 (i.e. £200 plus £40 plus £48 plus £58).

January 1st:— Extra gross profit £115 approximately (i.e. $33\frac{1}{3}\%$ of £346).
    Extra *net* profit say £69.

The extra *net* profit of £69, invested in stock, now gives us a total extra stock over the whole year of £415 (i.e. £200 plus £40 plus £48 plus £58 plus £69).
 In short, our extra £200 stock could, from the beginning of one year to the beginning of the next year, have become £415, and the process I have outlined might continue over further periods.

It is evident that these ideas and figures on the reinvestment of profit in stock will repay very close thought. The example given is for illustration only and you can work out figures which would be realistic for your own business, according to your profit margins and rate of turnover.

Unsaleable goods held in stock are very expensive luxuries; the example given indicates how much you could afford to reduce the price of unsaleable goods and use the resultant cash to recoup yourself.

There are few businesses where cash found by dealing with surplus stock cannot be used to finance additional sales. In the rare cases where it cannot be so employed, the money may be used in other ways in or out of the business; to leave it in dead stock is quite unprofitable.

If buying discount parcels for an extra few % gross profit is restricting your stock variety of selling lines, and leaving you with surplus stock, then you are sacrificing a large amount of profit for a small one. This sacrifice is caused by not controlling stock and by failure to invest money to most advantage.

Chapter 9

MAIN PRINCIPLES

The following main principles are well worth keeping in front of you:—

1. Sales, actual and prospective, are the key to purchases and stock requirements. To know your market is to find the true basis for your business activities.

2. Grouping of merchandise according to importance and frequency of stock checking, ensures that you put first things first and give most attention to the *vital* goods.

3. Budgeting ahead for purchases enables you to watch your capital investment and can help you avoid having your money tied up in slow-moving lines at the expense of the staple goods. To know your commitments in advance is a powerful aid in making arrangements with your bank or any other backers.

4. Consider every business step from the angle of what it will cost to carry out and what it can be expected to add to your pure profit.

5. You and your staff should never forget that the customer is the source of your livelihood. Any system must have in mind the increase of pure profit through *service* to the customer, the degree and type of service she wants and will pay for.

YOUR NOTES:-

Chapter 10

EFFICIENCY PRINCIPLES in STOCK CONTROL Etc.

Efficiency I define as the achievement of goals with the smallest amount of resources. Only you can decide what your own goals are, what you want stock control to do for you, but most of us in business aim, I suggest, to make the optimum profit from our stock.

Why do I write "optimum" and not "maximum" profit? It is because the biggest immediate profit might not help us to make the most profit over a longer period of time. Most business people aim to stay in business long-term and to continue to make profits. We are unwise to snatch at "quick in and out" profit unless of course this is our chosen goal.

Furthermore we have to take into account human moral and ethical factors in our business, sometimes because the law forces us to, sometimes because we feel we must. Profits, short term, could often be higher if we were quite unscrupulous about our duties to society.

When we look at efficiency we need to view the effects of our decisions on those outside our shop as well as on those inside. Everything we do affects our customers, our suppliers and others. If we waste resources, money, time, labour, we damage the community economy along with our own business.

Do we arrange stock with the customers' convenience in mind or to simplify our stock control? If we cut down on our delivery service how are we switching the cost of this? If we delay payment to suppliers shall we in the end make it impossible for them to continue to serve us efficiently? How far can we go in considering others? Can we run our shop so that our suppliers and customers and ourselves can all live and prosper?

Efficiency in the routine and the mechanics of stock control should set us free—free to spend more of ourselves and of our resources on our prime function. This prime function is to know or to find out what the consumer wants and to make a profit as a result. Efficiency should free us to work on market research, to influence people's wants, to anticipate them, to identify wants even before people are aware of them.

In my experience, retailers in general do not realise how important their part can be in market research. And manufacturers also tend to undervalue the retailer's key position.

Here for your consideration are some practical suggestions about efficiency; make your own additions. Think about the following:—

(A)   in relation to your stock policies.

(B)   in relation to your business as a whole.

Stock matters must be treated as linked with other factors in retailing

1.   *WAGES AND SALARIES:* Are you "saving" money on staff in cash directly but losing it through having untrained inefficient staff, staff who miss sales, staff who fail to report special requests, who are slack about ordering? Is the true cost of your "saving" a health cost to you? Are you paying in worry, in unnecessary labour, because you cannot delegate?

Would you sooner have extra years of business life at a little less annual profit, if in fact this is the choice? I suggest that in many cases higher paid and better-treated staff would *increase* your profit as well as improve your health and your chances of avoiding a coronary.

2.   *INVOICES & STATEMENTS:* Do you get your invoice with the goods? If not, why not? Who pays for the doubled labour of checking delivery notes as well as invoices? And why are statements necessary if both parties to a business transaction keep proper records?

3.   *RECORDS.* Do you or your staff repeatedly look up 'phone numbers, addresses, etc. in 'phone directories and elsewhere? Is information you want continually, always to hand and up to date? Have you ever had any professional specialist advice about filing systems?

4.   *CORRESPONDENCE ETC.* Very often a handwritten letter or memo can be quicker, cheaper, more effective, than typing. A triplicate book of memos leaves you with a record in *date* order in the book, plus a copy to file in the appropriate file. A quadruplicate system allows you to send

your correspondent a top *and* a carbon so that the reply can come back to you on the carbon. You can easily have special memo forms made so that it is quick and simple for a reply to be sent to you. Keep your secretary's typing work to a minimum and use her or his services in other ways as well.

Keep down the cost of mistakes and queries by using short pithy memos with the basic facts. Keep a simple suspense follow-up system. If someone else's mistakes cost you money and time, try and get them to pay as much of the cost as possible. And be fair if you are the one at fault.

If you have a complaint against say a supplier and you do not get prompt attention, go to the top, 'phone the Chairman or Managing Director or, better, get them to 'phone you back.

And deal *quickly* with incoming matters; it saves time almost always. If you keep putting off decision and action you can spend more time picking up the threads of the matter again and again than it would take to get it cleared up. And putting things off increases stress.

5. *TIME:* Check on time spent at board meetings, on seeing representatives, and so forth. Work out the cost of your time and relate time spent on anything to the importance and value of the matter in hand. Three or four directors devoting half an hour to discussing a new bike for the delivery boy—this kind of thing happens.

6. *COMMUNICATIONS:* Have you given your staff clear instructions, *in writing*, about ordering procedure, about dealing with shortages, complaints etc.? Do you have a copy of every order you place, however placed?

7. *TRAINING:* Does your staff training include training to buy as well as to sell?

8. *WORK STUDY AND MARKET RESEARCH:* Have you gone into the part your staff might play in these key activities?

9. *ACCOUNTS ETC.:* How soon after your financial year end do you see your accounts? How soon after that do you study them and *use* the

information? Speak with your accountant and find out what you can do to ensure that when you peruse your accounts it is not old history you are looking at. What are you doing about interim accounts, linked with a budget control system, however simple?

10. *THE DIARY AND THE BOARD:* Judging by the number of business and other people who promise and then forget, diaries are not used enough. Make a note and do not cross through until done. A large white board will serve as a planner for your year's activities at a glance; it can be a valuable time saver so you don't have to flick through your diary every time you want to see whether you are free, for a holiday or a conference.

These things are obvious, most useful, cheap and *neglected.*

11. *RUBBER STAMPS, STANDARD FORMS AND LETTERS, ETC.:* Use these to economise on your *writing* time. Look into the costs and benefits of any machine aids appropriate in your business. Consider money, but also time and mental stress. Calculators, automatic weighing and counting devices, copiers, closed circuit television, computers, can all contribute to efficiency if used aright.

Now add, I suggest, points especially applicable in your type of shop:—

12. . . . .

13. . . . .

14. . . . .

To conclude these notes:— Remember the management principle of *delegation.* Your own most important functions should be human relations, financial control, market research, marketing, buying, selling; these are the keys to stocking policies and systems. And all the points listed and any you yourself add should be related both to your stock policies and to your whole business.

See whether you can delegate either INSIDE or OUTSIDE your shop or shops such activities as book-keeping, V.A.T. returns, invoice checking, wages. Have you considered what expenses and worries specialists outside your own firm might be able to relieve you of? And make sure you inter-relate information from your *stock* system and information your books and accounts provide on sales, purchases, etc.

FINALLY, as standards of efficiency are *comparative, relative*, I recommend that you make full use of any interfirm comparison scheme available within your branch of retailing.

YOUR NOTES:-